ALSO BY MAUREEN MURDOCK

Fathers' Daughters: Breaking the Ties That Bind
The Heroine's Journey: Woman's Quest for Wholeness
The Heroine's Journey Workbook: A Map for Every Woman's Quest
Spinning Inward: Using Guided Imagery with Children for
  Learning, Creativity, and Relaxation
Unreliable Truth: On Memoir and Memory

MYTHMAKING

SELF-DISCOVERY AND THE
TIMELESS ART OF MEMOIR

MAUREEN MURDOCK

SHAMBHALA

Shambhala Publications, Inc.
2129 13th Street
Boulder, Colorado 80302
www.shambhala.com

Cover art: Book illustration by Katrina Noble
Cover and interior design: Katrina Noble

9 8 7 6 5 4 3 2 1

First Edition
Printed in the United States of America

Shambhala Publications makes every effort to print on acid-free, recycled paper.
Shambhala Publications is distributed worldwide by Penguin Random House, Inc., and its subsidiaries.

LIBRARY OF CONGRESS CATALOGING-IN-PUBLICATION DATA
Names: Murdock, Maureen, author.
Title: Mythmaking: self-discovery and the timeless art of memoir / Maureen Murdock.
Other titles: Self-discovery and the timeless art of memoir
Description: First edition. | Boulder, Colorado: Shambhala, [2024] | Includes bibliographical references.
Identifiers: LCCN 2023012086 | ISBN 9781645471943 (trade paperback)
Subjects: LCSH: Autobiography—Psychological aspects. | Autobiography—Authorship. | Myth.
Classification: LCC CT25 .M85 2024 | DDC 920—dc23/eng/20230516
LC record available at https://lccn.loc.gov/2023012086

For Bill

Contents

Acknowledgments

In 1990 I was teaching a creative writing course in the UCLA Extension Writers' Program entitled "The Hero/Heroine's Journey," having just published my book *The Heroine's Journey*. I wanted to look at the theme of the mythic journey through the lens of memoir, but I couldn't find any memoirs in my local bookstore. Autobiographies yes, but no memoirs. Not until Mary Karr's *The Liars' Club* and Frank McCourt's *Angela's Ashes* were published in the mid-1990s.

Since then, there has been an explosion of published memoirs, and I have had the privilege to teach many memoirists. I'd like to acknowledge the writers in my Los Angeles Monday Morning Memoir group: Brooke Anderson, Ruth Bochner, Jackie Connolly, Marilyn Davis, Bairbre Dowling, Dorothy Huebel, Hillary Krieger, and Janet Smith; and the writers in my Santa Barbara Wednesday and Thursday Morning Memoir groups: Julie Bloomer, Carolyn Butcher, Barbara Crofford, Peggy Garrity, Deb Gunther, Olivia Harris, Genie Hoyne, Molly Jordan Koch, Hilary Krieger, Peggy Lamb, Wendy Lukomski, Christine Lyon, Vicki Riskin, Jackie Toth, and Jana Zimmer.

I had the opportunity to co-teach "Myth and Memoir" to graduate students with Dennis Slattery at Pacifica Graduate Institute, and for the past five years I have had the honor to teach with Jennifer Leigh Selig in "Writing Down the Soul," the memoir course she created. I'd also like to acknowledge my students and fellow teachers at the International Women's

Writing Guild, in particular Myra Shapiro, Susan Tiberghien, and June Gould. Brooke Warner of She Writes Press has been an inspiration to many women memoirists, including myself and my students who have published their books with her. Susan E. King and my granddaughters Ella Murdock Gardner and Gillian Murdock read early drafts of this book and offered their insights. Bill Dial has always been the best partner a writer could have with his patience and support. My brilliant editor at Shambhala, Breanna Locke, had the wisdom to see the possibilities in a guidebook about myth and memoir that you now have in your hands: memoirists are *truly* contemporary mythmakers.

Introduction

I have always loved reading memoirs and started teaching memoir writing over thirty years ago. In the 1980s, I became intrigued by the popularity of Bill Moyers's series *Joseph Campbell and the Power of Myth*. I had worked and studied with Campbell during the late 1970s and early 1980s when he taught in California, and like many other Campbellites, I was captivated by his ability to weave together stories, legends, and images from an expansive range of cultures and find a common thread. His writings on the pervasive power of myth in modern life offered me a new way to look at the repeating patterns lived out in each generation, and I incorporated his theories—and his challenge to live our lives as if "you were what you really are"—into my teaching of myth and memoir writing in the UCLA Extension Writers' Program in the early 1990s and later in the 2000s at Pacifica Graduate Institute in Santa Barbara.

Myths may be stories about gods and goddesses, heroes and heroines, origins and mores lived by the ancestors and handed down to us, but there is also a recurring enactment of the narrative pattern embedded in the story. The once-upon-a-time is also now a living event. It is this twofold aspect of then and now that fulfills the timeless collective essence of the myth and proves essential to the writing of memoir, as memoirists bring forward events of the past and reenact them, giving them form and significance in writing.

WHY WRITE MEMOIR?

We all need to tell our story and to understand our story. We all need to understand our passage from birth to life and then to death. We need for our life to signify, to touch the eternal, to understand the mysterious, to find out who we are.[1] We are compelled to listen to the stories of others because we want to see ourselves reflected in them. Grappling with uncertainty and ambiguity in our own lives, we seek direction in the memoirs of others.

Those of us who write memoir write it to figure out the meaning of events in our lives. Making meaning is key to the writing of memoir; otherwise, we could write a short story, a travelogue, a political essay, flash fiction. We mine our memories and emotions to make sense of the disparate episodes in our lives, tracing the evolution of several different selves in the process. Memoir writing has the magic of not just telling a story about the individual who writes the memory but also touching some aspect of the universal. In that way, memoir has the power to be healing for both writer and reader, as will be explored more in chapter 9. Memoirists are our contemporary mythmakers.

I was happy to hear Jackie, one of my eighty-something-year-old female students, say, "I never realized my life had value until I wrote my memoir. I have much more appreciation for myself now."

Jackie's comment illustrates the value of writing memoir. While it benefits writers to examine these themes in their writing, one need not be a writer to benefit from this book. Those who feel stuck or reluctant to write about themselves will find thought-provoking inspiration and validation in this book, while those simply looking to explore writing as a tool for self-exploration and therapeutic reflection will gain a deeper understanding of their inner selves. As a psychotherapist, I have noticed that many of my memoir students gain more insight into the workings of their psyches by writing memoir than they do in therapy.

OVERVIEW

I invite you to explore your personal mythology as you respond to the suggestions at the end of each chapter of this book. Together we'll look at excerpts from contemporary memoirists who, perhaps unconsciously, reflect Campbell's domains of myth in their writing. These published memoirs provide examples to help you identify and write about archetypal themes in your own life. You will also find a recurring section called "Crafting Your Memoir" at the end of each chapter that will address some of the practical aspects of writing memoir, such as sensory details and character development. I hope you will find value in thinking about the writing prompts at the end of each chapter; they are there to jog your memory and inspire self-reflection. They offer a structure and a starting point for you to make meaning from your life through the process of writing. Chapter 1 sets our foundation for exploring the memoir genre through the lens of ancient myths and archetypes. Chapters 2 through 5 explore questions that are central to memoir: Who am I? Who are my people? What is my journey? What is my purpose? Chapters 6 through 10 invite you to reflect on archetypal themes such as wounding and the body, home and homecoming, exile and immigration, loss, and spirituality.

HOW TO USE THIS BOOK

When you read the writing prompts at the end of each chapter, see if any of them pique your interest. You might not want to write a response to them right away, but consider keeping a journal or notebook to jot down ideas to explore in the future. There might be a particular myth or archetype you wish to explore further. I keep a "process" file on my computer where I write ideas that are inspired by reading the memoirs quoted in this book. Consider reading the books listed in the bibliography to learn how different writers approach the writing of memoir. You can also read more about the myths discussed in this book from the works listed in the "References on Myths" section of the bibliography.

My wish is for this book to deepen your understanding of the memoir genre and inspire you to feel empowered enough to put pen to your own life story.

PART ONE

ESTABLISHING YOUR MYTH FOUNDATIONS

1

•

ANCIENT MYTH, CONTEMPORARY MEMOIR

The most we can do is to dream the myth onward and
give it a modern dress.
—CARL G. JUNG, "The Archetypes
and the Collective Unconscious"

MYTHS AND FOLKTALES are the oldest stories we have.
They have been handed down to us to show us how people
have lived their lives for thousands of years—how they developed their mores and beliefs and created the rituals to celebrate
life and death. Our ancestors sat around the fire at night and
told each other stories about Helios, the sun god who drove
his chariot each day from east to west to light up the sky. They
told of Selene, the moon goddess, who drove her white chariot
across the sky each night and created each phase of the moon
as it waxed and waned.

Tales of gods and goddesses, heroes and demons have
been the time-honored way of examining psychological

characteristics and patterns of human behavior. Our distant ancestors looked to the sun, moon, and stars for guidance and direction. Our contemporaries pin their hopes and dreams on meditation, organized religion, or psychotherapy. Although practices vary and change, the underlying motivation remains the same: we have always, as a species, yearned for meaning. The Mormon environmentalist Terry Tempest Williams writes, "It is our nature to create meaning and make myths out of our lives. Each religion creates an anthology of stories, some oral, some written, in an attempt to make the sacred concrete. The Bible. The Torah. The Koran. The Hopi Prophecy. The Book of Mormon. Creation cosmologies around the world deliver us to a place of compassion and reverence. We see the world whole, even holy."[1]

Like myth, memoir presupposes that there is a certain unity to human experience, that we all share similar hopes, dreams, and desires. When we tell the story of how and where we grew up, who our parents were, how the significant people in our lives influenced us, what challenges and obstacles we faced, and how we dealt with triumph and failure, we are locating ourselves within an ancient human tradition of storytelling and meaning making. Memoirs help us find meaning in our lives by showing us how our lives fit into a larger mythic pattern. When a writer recounts a memory about themselves, they are talking about all of us to some degree. The essence of memoir is to participate in the writer's struggle to achieve some understanding of the events, traumas, and triumphs of their personal recollection.

Memoir often gets confused with autobiography and biography. Memoir is not a linear autobiographical account of a fully lived life but rather a *selected* aspect of the writer's life, written from their point of view. Rather than simply recounting an incident or memory from their life, the memoirist both tells the story and tries to make meaning out of it. When they recognize that certain episodes in their life reflect a particular mythic pattern (like the stages of the hero/heroine's journey or the parent-child relationship), they will appreciate their experience on a larger scale, reminding them they are part of a shared global community.

ARCHETYPES

In every society, mythmakers start with an archetype. *Archetypes* are invisible primary patterns, such as the parent-child bond, which we cannot normally perceive in the moment but whose energy propels us. The mythmaker creates a specific story that expresses the invisible pattern. But the mythmaker is inventing only the current manifestation of a mythic theme that already exists unconsciously in the collective.

For example, in ancient literature, Odysseus's journey across the seas was invented or appropriated to serve as a Greek expression of heroism. In the twenty-first-century cultural lexicon of film, the journey of the orphan Rey in *Star Wars: The Force Awakens* was invented to serve as a Western ideal of heroism. Both heroes represent something of our own psychological journey. The myth of Odysseus is passed on from generation to generation by acculturation, but the hero archetype is passed on through constantly repeated experiences of human existence.

When you reflect upon a myth, think about how the action or plot reflects something in your own life, your own story. For example, how have you been loved like Psyche and Eros? The structure of the myth of Psyche and Eros involves separation, a loss of innocence, trials, failure, and despair. But at the end, Psyche faces her humanity and gains a more mature understanding of love. The first love of many young people reflects at least some elements of this structure.

You might also look at how you have felt betrayed like Persephone by her father, Zeus—or like Britney Spears, a modern-day Persephone, by her father, Jamie. How have you been abducted into the underworld by Hades? How have you abducted others? Have you overcome trials in your life to return to safety, as Odysseus did on his winding journey home?

It is difficult to see your own story while you're living it. But if a person looks to a particular mythic pattern for direction, it not only helps them understand their path but also gives them the opportunity to see themselves in relation to others and to their place in the world. It illuminates why certain challenges occur. It gives them comfort to know that others have experienced what they have lived.

Our lives are made up of millions of moments, each bringing small terrors, beauties, and revelations; each imbued with its own significance. With so many stories and experiences to tell, it can be difficult to know where to start your memoir. Myth can provide a starting point and a road map. The dragons and demons encountered along your journey are but reflections of unresolved issues in your life.

What is the story or the narrative that just walked into the room with you? What is the story you tell about yourself, your family, your culture; and what meaning do you make from the story you tell? The story you tell becomes the story you live. As the American memoirist and educator Patricia Hampl explains, "Because everyone 'has' a memoir, we all have a stake in how such stories are told. For we do not, after all, simply have experience; we are entrusted with it. We must do something—make something—with it."[2]

CAMPBELL'S FOUR DOMAINS OF MYTH

Although not every memoir reflects a mythic theme, most memoir writers unconsciously reveal mythic themes in their desire to find meaning in their lives. This is because inquiry lies at the heart of both memoir and mythology, and both arose from a human need for connection.

Joseph Campbell proposed four domains of myth, which I think also address the tenants of memoir:

Who am I? How did I come about?
Who are my people, my family? To whom do I belong?
Where am I going? How do I make my way?
What is my purpose? Where do I fit in within the greater scheme of things?

I suspect that one of the reasons memoir is so popular today is because many memoirs address one or more of these questions. Certainly the first domain—"Who am I? How did I come about?"—is at the core of every memoir. In her memoir *Inheritance: A Memoir of Genealogy, Paternity, and Love*, Dani Shapiro explores the crisis of identity she experienced when she found out, through a DNA test at age fifty-four, that her father was not actually her birth father. If the father she grew up with is not her actual father, Shapiro wonders, who is *she*? She is afraid that she has become unknowable not only to herself but also to others. "My body wasn't the body I had believed it to be for fifty-four years. My face wasn't my face. . . . If my body wasn't my body and my face wasn't my face, who was I?"[3] Her memoir becomes her origin myth.

When the energies present in the older, mythical tales are captured in newer, contemporary stories, modern readers can still experience an archetypally lived event. We access the archetypal through the personal. For example, in *The Year of Magical Thinking*, Joan Didion describes waiting in their apartment for her husband, John, to return from the dead after his sudden heart attack. Her inability to accept the finality of his death recalls Orpheus's vain attempt to reverse the death of his beloved Eurydice and bring her back from Hades. If she could, Didion, too, would have made the journey to the underworld to reclaim John. Didion writes about her need to spend the night of her husband's death alone.

> Of course I knew John was dead. Of course I had already delivered the definitive news to his brother and to my brother and to Quintana's husband. *The New York Times* knew. *The Los Angeles Times* knew. Yet I was myself in no way prepared to accept this news as final: there was a level on which I believed that what had happened remained reversible. . . . I needed to be alone so that he could come back.[4]

The psychologist Carl G. Jung believed that every society has specific stories that express archetypal themes, such as the death of a loved one, but in each society the stories emerge from manifestations of already mythic material.[5] The yearning for a figure to embody the archetype remains; the persona changes. While Eurydice embodies the ancient archetype of the dead spouse, Didion's husband John embodies the current persona.

The Mexican American memoirist Brando Skyhorse wrote *Take This Man* to describe his search for his birth father who had abandoned him when he was three years old. In Homer's *Odyssey*, Telemachus, too, was inspired to go in search of his father, the Greek hero Odysseus, who abandoned him when he was still an infant. Like Telemachus, Skyhorse's contemporary search to find his father describes the deep longing one has for one's people and the desire of a son to truly know his absent father.

> I was three years old when my father abandoned me and my mother in my grandmother's house atop a crooked hill on Portia Street in a Los Angeles neighborhood called Echo Park. My mother, Maria Teresa, a Mexican who wanted to be an American Indian, transformed me into Brando Skyhorse, a full-blooded American Indian Brave. . . . Her deception was so good, or so obvious, she fooled each of her five husbands, our neighbors, her friends, my elementary school vice principal, even me. I lived most of my childhood without knowing who I really was. All I knew was the power in my own name: *"Brando Skyhorse? That's beautiful."*[6]

The best-selling author Cheryl Strayed—whose chosen surname even reflects one aspect of her self-invention—wrote *Wild* not only to document her 1,100-mile solo trek along the Pacific Crest Trail but also to come to terms with the death of her mother. Her memoir resonated with readers around the world because her story was archetypal: like Persephone who was abducted from her mother, Demeter, into the underworld by Hades, the loss of her mother and the pain of separation plunged Strayed into a deep descent. Four years later, her journey from the Mojave Desert through California and Oregon to Washington ultimately healed her.

All stories consist of a few common structural elements found universally in myths, fairy tales, dreams, and movies. Think about each character in a dream or myth as an aspect of yourself. Characters such as a young hero, wise old man, or wicked witch are the same figures who appear in your dreams and fantasies. That's why myths and most stories have a ring of psychological truth to them. The universal power of myth is that they deal with universal questions.

When you look at your particular story through the lens of myth or archetype, you will recognize how the patterns of your life mirror life patterns of others. The details may be different, but the themes are similar. There is comfort knowing you are not alone; you tread a path well worn by the ancients. Wisdom and insight come from that recognition. In the chapters that follow, we will explore specific examples of themes central to myth and memoir.

CRAFTING YOUR MEMOIR

THE STARTING PLACE

Memoir is not a linear autobiographical account of a fully lived life but rather a *selected* aspect of your life, written from your point of view. Your memory of an event or a particular time in your life may be nothing more than a fleeting image at first. Start with that image, whatever it is, and follow it. It's a starting place, like the beginning of any journey. You will be surprised by what memories begin to emerge as you start writing. No event is too small or too insignificant to write about. It's *how* you write about it that matters. Write with as much detail as possible. Where were you at the time? How old were you? Who was with you or were you alone? What were you doing? How did you feel?

What was going on? Details are important, particularly sensory details. They lead to feelings. Your memory might be the smell of lilacs in early spring or the taste of warm toast, the soft texture of your puppy's fur or a movement of your bedroom curtain in the breeze at night when you were alone. In discussing her own remembering process in "The Site of Memory," the Noble Prize–winning author Toni Morrison writes, "The image comes first and tells me what the 'memory' is about."[7]

WRITING PROMPTS

GETTING STARTED

1. Is there a particular ancient myth or mythological character with whom you identify?
2. Perhaps you recognize something of yourself in that character's journey?
3. Of Campbell's four domains of myth, described on page 5, which are you most drawn to?
4. Archetypal themes such as separation, loss of innocence, trials, failure, betrayal, love, and despair are often present in myth and memoir. Which archetypes would your story include?
5. A personal myth addresses itself to our past, present, and future as well as our identity and purpose in the world. What is your personal myth?
6. What is the family myth handed down by your parents and grandparents?
7. What part of the family myth do you carry?

2

·

WHO AM I?
CREATION MYTHS

Like Creation stories everywhere, cosmologies are
a source of identity and orientation to the world.
They tell us who we are. We are inevitably shaped by
them no matter how distant they may be from our
consciousness.

   —ROBIN WALL KIMMERER, *Braiding Sweetgrass*

THE BOTANIST Robin Wall Kimmerer tells us that creation
stories offer us "a glimpse into the worldview of a people, of
how they understand themselves, their place in the world, and
the ideals to which they aspire."[1] When we read and study creation myths, we begin to understand that they describe not the
origin of the world but rather the origin of humankind's conscious awareness of the world. An awakening to consciousness
comes out of an unconscious state. A similar thing happens
when we write memoir. We become conscious of memories and
emotions that have laid fallow for many years and how they
affect us in the present. Our inner journey reveals itself.

One of my favorite creation myths is the Northwest Coast Haida legend of Raven, the "Haida Trickster." There are several variations of the myth. In the Swiss psychologist Marie-Louise von Franz's telling, "The first living creature on the land was called Father Raven because he created all life on earth and is the origin of everything."[2]

Bill Reid, the Northwest Coast artist who created a monumental yellow cedar sculpture of *The Raven and the First Men* for the British Columbia Museum of Anthropology, tells the origin story this way:

> Raven sat crouching in the darkness when he suddenly awoke to consciousness and discovered himself. He did not know where he was or how he had come into being, but he breathed and had life, he lived. Suddenly he saw an extraordinary clamshell at his feet and protruding from it were a number of small creatures. The Raven coaxed them to leave the shell to join him in his wonderful world. Some were hesitant at first, but eventually, overcome by curiosity, they crept or scrambled out from the partly open clamshell.
>
> They were very strange creatures, two-legged like the Raven. There the resemblance ended. They had no glossy feathers, no thrusting beak, their skin was pale and they were naked except for their long, black hair on their round, flat-featured heads. Instead of strong wings they had stick-like appendages that waved and fluttered constantly. They were the original Haidas, the first humans.[3]

Raven had not intended to create a human being; he claims no higher understanding of his *own* creation, and he confesses his astonishment that his actions led to the emergence of these strange little stick creatures, these first human beings. Thus Raven is an unconscious creator, one who creates the world through uncovering what is already latent, both literally and figuratively. He reveals humanity by coaxing them out from under the clamshell.

Like Raven, memoirists create through discovery. The writer remembers various moments in their life, puts them down on paper, and becomes conscious that these fragments make up their life. To do this, they must delve beneath the firm crust of memory to bring light to the meaning beneath. Memoirs that reflect the mythic theme of "Who am I?" look at the issues of origins, birth, naming, identity, and the initial wound of separation from the mother.

ORIGINS

The Cuban American memoirist Flor Fernandez Barrios writes about how the events of her birth and the name given to her at birth defined, in many ways, the trajectory of her life. Barrios was born in Cuba during a thunder-and-lightning storm. Her grandmother Patricia, a curandera, named her Flor for St. Thérèse of Lisieux, "the Little Flower." Patricia prayed to the saint to ensure a safe birth and promised the saint that Flor, too, would become a healer. From the moment Flor drew her first breath, she carried the myths and rituals of her Cubo-African culture.

In her memoir *Blessed by Thunder*, Barrios discovers not only the gift of her name but also the calling it invites her to answer or to reject. She was born in the town of Cabaiguan, Cuba, in the middle of a hurricane. A couple minutes past midnight, as Barrios was entering the world, a thunderbolt struck nearby with such force that the lights went out in the hospital. Her grandmother always maintained that the storm was prophetic, a symbol of Barrios's destiny:

"Negrita," she would say to me, "you have a don, a gift. Never forget that thunder greeted you into this life." Then she would explain that thunder and lightning were the powers of the Yoruba deity Changó, known as Saint Barbara in the Catholic religion.

My name is Flor Teresa, but my Grandmother Patricia always called me Negrita, which means "little black one." It was her way of expressing affection and love for me, her favorite grandchild, the one she believed would carry on the tradition of healing and become a curandera, like her.[4]

Barrios's grandmother taught her the healing rituals of her culture until she and her family fled Castro's Cuba when she was fifteen. In order to assimilate into a new culture in Southern California, Barrios rejected the rituals and healing herbs of her grandmother. However, many years later, as a practicing psychologist, she realized she had never truly abandoned the healing wisdom of her ancestors. She had given them a different form by treating patients as a psychotherapist. The circumstances of her birth became her origin myth. But, of course, she didn't realize this until she wrote her memoir.

Some people, like Barrios, write memoir to discover what their obligation is to their ancestors. In writing about her parents who had survived Auschwitz, Jana Zimmer, one of my memoir students, discovered that she had unconsciously chosen her profession as an attorney and crafted her entire life to make up for the losses her family experienced in the Holocaust. She has given me permission to quote from this piece written in class, which later appeared in her book *Chocolates from Tangier*:

My parents, Josef and Klara, met in Prague on my mother's birthday in October 1945. Each was the sole survivor (of the concentration camps) of their family. They had barely begun to build a new life together when the Czech communists, capitalizing on their stage-managed "liberation" of Prague were "elected" in 1948. We fled to Canada as refugees in December, arriving in Montreal effectively penniless.

Thirty years after our escape from Czechoslovakia, I became a lawyer, intent on doing something important enough to make up for my family's losses, enough to justify my own existence. I had no religious training, and no familiarity with the Torah growing up, but apparently the admonition of Deuteronomy 16:20 had taken root in me: "Justice, Justice shalt thou pursue."[5]

Zimmer and her parents were forcibly torn away from their country, experiencing the wound of loss not only of property but of their culture. Jana grew up feeling the need to rectify her parents' losses. Do you feel that you have an obligation to your ancestors? For example, perhaps you feel pressure to succeed if your ancestors worked hard for you to be born into a position of privilege. Or maybe you make an effort in your daily life to honor the rich cultural or religious heritage from your family's past, or you work to keep your family name alive. Is there unfinished business for you to complete?

IDENTITY THROUGH LOSS

In *Why Be Happy When You Could Be Normal?* the British memoirist Jeanette Winterson writes about her experience of being torn away from her mother at birth. Winterson, who was adopted by an intolerant adoptive mother, writes about the emotional wound created by her physical separation from her mother's body marked by the severing of the umbilical cord. Winterson's memoir recounts her desperate attempt to find her birth mother as she deals with constant denigration by her adoptive mother, Mrs. Winterson, who rejects her for being gay. Unable to accept or understand her adopted daughter's sexuality, Mrs. Winterson asks, "Why be happy when you could be normal?"

Winterson tells the reader that she has always been interested in stories of disguise and mistaken identity, of naming and knowing. She asks us how we're recognized and how we recognize ourselves and answers her own question by placing her wound within the context of a larger mythical framework:

> In the Odyssey, Odysseus, for all his adventures and far-flung wandering, is always urged to "remember the return." The journey is about coming home.
>
> When he reaches Ithaca the place is in uproar with unruly suitors for his hard-pressed wife. Two things happen: his dog scents him, and his wife recognizes him by the scar on his thigh.
>
> She feels the wound.[6]

> All my life I have worked from the wound. To heal it would mean an end to one identity—the defining identity.[7]

After she searches for and finds her birth mother, Winterson comes to terms with the fact she will always search for belonging—for love, identity, home, and mother. She writes, "I have a theory that every time you make an important choice, the part of you left behind continues the other life you could have had."[8]

Is there a way you identify with Winterson? How do you relate to your family of origin? Is there a wound that needs healing? Perhaps you lost your mother or father at an early age; or you experienced a debilitating illness; or you moved away from your best friend; or you had difficulty adjusting to a new culture; or you were confused about your gender or sexuality. Notice how these wounds from childhood affect your sense of belonging.

SECRECY AS IDENTITY

Some memoirists identify so intensely with a parent that their own identity becomes subordinate, subsumed into the life of their magnetic, elevated progenitor. In *The Bishop's Daughter*, the poet Honor Moore writes about her idealization of her father, much like the Greek goddess Athena, the archetype of the daughter who identifies with her father.

Athena's very birth defined her as her father's daughter. She sprang out of Zeus's head as a full-grown woman, wearing flashing gold armor, holding a sharp spear in one hand, and emitting a mighty war cry. Following this dramatic birth, Athena associated herself only with Zeus, acknowledging him as her sole parent. The goddess never acknowledged her mother, Metis. In fact, Athena seemed ignorant of the fact that she had a mother. When Metis was pregnant with Athena, Zeus tricked her into becoming small and swallowed her. It was predicted that Metis would have two very special children: a daughter equal to Zeus in courage and wise counsel; and a son, a boy of all-conquering heart who would become king of gods and men. By swallowing Metis, Zeus thwarted fate and took over her attributes as his own.[9]

Like Athena, Honor Moore was in thrall of her father, the Episcopalian bishop of New York. At Easter, as the congregation waits in silence, her father enters the darkness of the Cathedral of St. John the Divine. With three resounding knocks on the door, it is as if God himself is entering:

And as we wait, the massive doors swing open, an ethereal shaft of sunlight floods the dark, the roar of the city breaks the gigantic quiet, and there . . . in a blaze of morning light, stands the tall figure of a man. My flesh-and-blood father, the bishop.

When I was a child, I accepted my father as a force of imagination that flared and burst and coruscated, an instrument of transformation. . . . My father had supernatural powers. His fate had determined my existence. I was something he had made and would continue to make . . . it took me decades to escape the enchantment of my father's priesthood.[10]

In her memoir, Moore divulges that her father was bisexual and had kept that secret from his family and congregation. Though she was criticized by her siblings for "outing" her father in her book after his death, she writes about how important it was to come to terms with her father's sexuality so that she could come to terms with her own. Her identity was merged with his.

I explained to [Emma] that I had been with women for fifteen years of my life and that telling the story of my father and myself was necessary to my understanding him, to altering the pattern of sexual unhappiness that I had inherited. I told her that I believed sexuality to be a crucial aspect of existence, that my father had considered sexuality and faith to coexist in the same realm of the spirit.[11]

When Moore learned that her father had a secret sexual life, she began to understand how her own sexual development had been tied up with his complicated erotic life. She writes about how important it was for her to understand the complexity of his relationships and what impact they had on her and her mother. Since she is a writer, "understanding meant telling."[12] For Moore, caring involved immersing herself in what wanted to remain untouched. And that led to "telling."

I imagine that in "telling," Moore violated her family's code of secrecy about her late father's sexuality. But despite criticism from her siblings, she needed to write her truth—not to cast aspersions on her father's memory but to make sense of her own closeted life, her secret relationships, and her innermost thoughts. Writing about family is always fraught with pitfalls. You want to be fair to your loved ones, but you also must be fair to yourself. In writing, we satisfy the intense urge to make sense of subjective experiences that are ours alone. Think about whether there is a secret that you have carried for your parents. Does that secret weigh upon you?

Whereas Moore attempts to disentangle her own identity from the all-consuming image of her father, the memoirist Dani Shapiro struggles to recreate herself after the father-daughter bond is irrevocably altered.

As a child, Dani Shapiro felt that she never "fit" in her Orthodox Jewish family. A blue-eyed, light-complexioned blond, she didn't look like either of her parents, who had dark complexions. It wasn't until she was fifty-four years old and compared her DNA with that of her stepsister that she discovered that her stepsister and she were not related; the man she believed to be her father was not, in fact, her biological father. In *Inheritance*, she writes,

> It turns out that it is possible to live an entire life—even an examined life, to the degree that I had relentlessly examined mine—and still not know the truth of oneself. . . . All my life I had known there was a secret. What I hadn't known: the secret was me.[13]

Perhaps it had been the unconscious yearning to unearth this secret that was always at the core of her identity as a writer:

> I am a spinner of narratives, a teller of tales. I have spent my life attempting to make meaning out of random events, to shape stories out of an accretion of senseless, chaotic detail. As a writer and a teacher of writing, this is what I do. . . . What never fails to draw me in, however, are secrets. Secrets within families. Secrets we keep out of shame, or self-protectiveness, or denial. Secrets and their corrosive power. Secrets we keep from one another in the name of love.[14]

Shapiro becomes, like Raven, an unconscious creator. She had not intended to become a fatherless daughter. Like Raven, she uncovers a new world for herself by discovering her actual birth father partly by accident. Had she never had a DNA test, she would never have unearthed the secret about her origins. Memoirists like Winterson, Moore, and Shapiro find secrecy at the core of their identities and write themselves into being.

CRAFTING YOUR MEMOIR

What are the pitfalls in writing memoir? When you begin to write a memoir, it is not unusual to doubt your memory. Did I get it right? Did it really happen the way I remember? Was it as bad (or as good) as I remember? Do I have a right to write about this? Whose story is mine to tell?

Family members will tell you that it didn't happen that way or they might even tell you that you weren't there. Hilary, one of my memoir students, wrote a fabulous memoir piece about skiing in the Alps with her six siblings as a ten-year-old. The family was living in Italy at the time during their father's yearlong sabbatical from teaching, and they went to Switzerland for Christmas. When Hilary shared the piece with her siblings, they laughed hysterically and her older brother said, "You weren't even there!" (She included their reaction in her memoir.)

When my book *Unreliable Truth* was first published, a woman came up to me at a book signing and questioned my use of the word *unreliable* in the title. I told her that I couldn't guarantee the factual truth of each event but that I had written it to the best of my recollection. I was sure of the emotional truth because it was my experience. She confessed that she, too, was writing a memoir and that she "had" the truth. The only truth. However, her brothers each said, "It didn't happen that way." When I told her it probably didn't happen that way for *them* because they had their own angle of perception, their own truth, she said, "No, I *have* the truth," and she walked away.

Memoir is not journalism, although some memoirists research the era in which they are writing—the music, politics, fashion, food, films, and so forth—to make their memoir as factually correct as possible. Trust your story. Write a scene and react to it on the page. Dialogue with your writer. List the judgments you have about yourself and get them out of the way. Write a letter from your present self to the person you were in the past that shows how you see your younger self now. Remind yourself of how old you were back then and the conditions in your family and in the culture at the time. Have compassion. Write knowing you can and will make changes later. Remember, writing it is not the same as publishing. Write to find out who you are.

Annie Ernaux, who received the 2022 Nobel Prize in Literature for her memoirs including *The Years*, says, "For me, writing was and remains a way to shed light on things that one feels but are unclear. Writing is a path to knowledge."[15]

WRITING PROMPTS

YOUR ORIGIN STORY

Use one or more of these prompts to inspire your writing:

1. Where were you born? How does your birthplace continue to inform your life today?
2. Flor Fernandez Barrios tells us she was named for

St. Thérèse, "the Little Flower." What were you told about your name?
3. How do you identify with your culture, race, gender?
4. What is your obligation to your ancestors?
5. What do you know about yourself to be true?
6. Has there been a secret you have carried for your parents? What is it and how has it affected you?
7. How does your story or memoir reflect current issues in your culture?

3

WHO ARE MY PEOPLE?

They are the tangled roots—thick, rich, and dark—
that bind me to the turning earth.

—DANI SHAPIRO, *Inheritance*

IN THE INTRODUCTION I suggested that both myth and memoir examine the important questions in life: Who am I? Who are my people? Where am I going? Where do I fit in within the greater scheme of things? In this chapter, we will look at the issues around family in memoir and myth.

The family we belong to anchors us. Our ancestors are the foundation upon which we build our lives. In writing memoir, we wrestle with them, empathize with them, try to understand them and come to terms with them. In speaking of her ancestors, Dani Shapiro writes, "They have been my territory—my obsession, you might even say. They are the tangled roots—thick, rich, and dark—that bind me to the turning earth. During younger years when I was lost—particularly after my dad's death—I used them as my inner compass."[1] We may not be conscious of their magnetic hold upon us, but we carry our ancestors' imprint. We push up against them to discover who we are. In *Leap*, Terry Tempest Williams writes, "Inside my veins, I feel the pulse of my people, those dead and those standing beside me, a pulse I will always be driven by, a pulse that registers as a murmur in my heart. I cannot escape my history, nor can I ignore the lineage that is mine. Most importantly, I don't want to."[2]

In *The Dragons, the Giant, the Women*, Wayétu Moore writes about her desperate longing for her mother, a student in New York at Columbia University on a Fulbright Scholarship while Wayétu is at home in Monrovia, Liberia. Wayétu, her father, sister, and grandparents are about to celebrate her fifth birthday when civil war breaks out in Monrovia. They are forced to flee their village on foot and hide in the forest for three weeks until they can find safety. The rituals and beliefs of their tribe are central to her narrative as the people of their village help each other escape. Wayétu makes connections between history and culture and the story of her family's plight as she describes her desire to be reunited with her mother. In one long unpunctuated sentence, she writes as the puzzled five-year-old as the family makes their escape:

> Where we going? I asked and nowhere was their answer though it did not make sense that we were making such a fuss on a journey that was not somewhere and "Where is Mam?" I asked and we are going to see her and I stopped counting the days forgot what Ma's voice sounded like.[3]

The entire memoir describes the pain of separation of daughter from mother and mother from daughter and the journey they both take to find each other in wartime, eventually to be reunited. It illustrates the archetypal pattern of the female quest in which mother and daughter separate and unite eternally. Moore's narrative reminded me of the mother-daughter relationship in the *Hymn to Demeter* written between 650 and 550 B.C.E. The ancient hymn describes the terror experienced by Demeter, who is not able to save her daughter from abduction into the underworld by Hades and the confusion and fear the young Persephone must have felt as she was lost to her known world.

In the beginning of the hymn, Persephone is gathering flowers in a meadow with her companions. She is attracted to a flower she has never seen before—a narcissus with one hundred blossoms. As she reaches out to pick it, the ground splits open and Hades comes forth in his golden chariot, grabs Persephone, and takes her to the underworld.

Demeter, who has been in an adjacent meadow, asks Persephone's companions what happened to her, but they saw nothing. Demeter searches for nine days and nine nights over land and sea, never stopping to eat, sleep, or bathe in her frantic search for her daughter. Helios tells Demeter that Hades grabbed Persephone and took her to the underworld to be his bride. He also tells her that the abduction had been sanctioned by Persephone's father, Zeus, the brother of Hades.

Demeter is furious. She feels not only grief and rage at the loss of her daughter but also betrayal by her consort, Zeus, who sanctioned this rape by his brother. While Demeter grieves, the earth lays barren and bleak. Wandering the countryside, she reaches Eleusis, where she sits by a well, exhausted and mournful. The daughters of Celeus, the ruler of Eleusis, come to the well and are drawn to Demeter. She tells them she is looking for work as a nursemaid, so they bring her home to their mother, Metanira, to help take care of their baby brother, Demophoon.

Each night, Demeter feeds the baby ambrosia and secretly holds him in a fire to make him immortal. One night, Demeter leaves the door open a crack and Metanira sees her lay the baby like a log on the fire. Furious because of Metanira's interference, Demeter rises to her full height, revealing her true identity and commands that a temple be built for her. Had Metanira not stopped Demeter from making Demophoon immortal, she would have robbed him of his humanity.

While Demeter sits there grieving for Persephone, nothing grows on earth. Famine spreads, and the gods and goddesses beseech Zeus to intervene. He sends Hermes, the messenger of the gods, to command Hades to return Persephone to Demeter so that she will restore growth and fertility on earth. As Persephone makes ready to leave the underworld, Hades circles her three times, placing a pomegranate seed in her mouth with each pass.

Hermes returns Persephone to Demeter, who asks her if she ate anything in the underworld. When Persephone admits that she has eaten Hades's seed, Demeter tells her that because she has eaten the seed, she will have to return to the underworld for a third of the year, during which time the earth will lay fallow. The remainder of the year she can stay with her mother and the earth will bear fruit.

The themes in this myth focus on abduction and betrayal, wandering and grief, and the desire to keep the idealized child alive. In the act of reaching out for the unknown—a fantastical narcissus—Persephone is snatched away from the meadow, from the innocence of adolescence, and plunges into darkness. Her descent transforms her into an adult. Had Persephone not made the journey to the underworld, she would have forever remained her mother's daughter. Her individuation from her mother occurs through her initiation and descent.

The female quest differs significantly from the male quests of Odysseus and Telemachus because the focus is on healing the wounding of the feminine psyche, culturally and person-ally, through an experience of descent and return. The daugh-ter's need to separate from the mother contrasts with the son's quest for the absent father for reconciliation and acceptance. Telemachus had many adventures in search of his father, most dramatically when he helped Odysseus fend off the suitors who had invaded their ancestral home demanding Penelope's hand in marriage. His is a coming-of-age narrative proving his worth as a man.

By viewing the myth of Demeter and Persephone from Demeter's perspective, one comes to understand mothering not just biologically but as a way of being in the world. Both Demeter and Wayétu's mother, Mam, embody the archetype of mother and how much of motherhood is loss—experiencing "the loss of a child as the loss of herself."[4]

Memoirs that focus on the mother-daughter relationship often reflect the archetypal theme of enmeshed relationships like that of Demeter and Persephone and the painful struggle for separation. J, a memoir student who gave me permission to quote her work about separating from her mother, writes, "All the stories I end up writing circle back somehow to me longing for her. Even when I wanted separation, I longed for her to help me separate, to initiate the separation, to mourn it, and then celebrate it with me like I imagined a normal mother would."[5] The memoirist Sven Birkerts writes, "The crisis of entanglement and the willful push for separation have to be seen as one of the central impulses in these narratives."[6]

LONGING FOR THE MOTHER

The Pulitzer Prize–winner Natasha Trethewey uses the met-aphor of the Persephone myth quite directly in her memoir

Memorial Drive. At nineteen years old, Natasha Trethewey lost her mother when her former stepfather shot and killed her. Thirty years later, when she is forty-nine, Trethewey returns for the first time to Memorial Drive in Atlanta to piece together memories of her life with her mother before she was murdered.

When they had first moved to Atlanta when she was a child, Trethewey picked a handful of yellow narcissi to give her mother as she dressed for her new job at the Mine Shaft club in Underground Atlanta. She rues the day she gave her mother the flowers:

> I know that I have picked them for her, a handful of yellow narcissi—the flowers planted, in the myth of mother and daughter, to lure Persephone to her doom: kidnapping by the lord of the underworld. She picks a bright flower and the earth splits open beneath her, taking her into its dark throat.
>
> It's as though I had rewritten the myth, passed the doom onto my mother as easily as I had handed her that rough bouquet of daffodils. That night descending to work beneath the city, my mother was already entering an underworld from which she would never fully emerge.[7]

Trethewey uses the metaphor of Persephone's initiation and descent to describe her own. She writes, "What matters is the transformative power of metaphor and the stories we tell ourselves about the arc and meaning of our lives. . . . What has changed is how I've understood what I saw, how I've come to interpret the metaphors inherent in my way of recalling the events."[8] The seduction of the narcissi becomes the vehicle for her own and her mother's descent.

The purpose of a memoir is not merely to record the events of one's life but to be conscious of how certain events in one's life have shaped that life and continue to shape and expand it. Memoir is not only a recollection of the past but also a way of defining oneself in the present. Writing memoir shows the writer becoming aware of creating themselves. As James Olney, the scholar of autobiography, explains in his book *Metaphors of Self*, "The self expresses itself by the metaphors it creates and projects. We do not see or touch the self, but we do see and touch its metaphors."[9] Trethewey writes the myth forward; she gives it a modern dress.

LEAVING HOME

The award-winning memoirist Sarah M. Broom wrote *The Yellow House*, set in New Orleans after the devastation of Hurricane Katrina, about the inexorable pull of home and family. The youngest of twelve children, Broom tells the story of her widowed mother's battle to keep the house and family intact in the face of decay and civic neglect. The archetypal obligation to tribe and place is reflected in Broom's struggle between leaving her mother and the remains of their battered home in New Orleans and constantly being drawn back. It is ten years since Hurricane Katrina took the Yellow House, yet Broom is still haunted by the image of her brother Carl babysitting ruins, sitting on the empty plot where their childhood home used to be.

On the evening of the second day, I arrive in New Orleans. I call Carl, who tells me to find him at the Yellow House, where we grew up. It was demolished a year after the water. None of us was there to see it go. When it came down, all seven of my siblings who lived in New Orleans were displaced. There are twelve of us in all, and I am the baby. We had all inherited from our mother the tendency, the need even, to make the things that belonged to us presentable, but even Carl could not put the house back together again. Instead, he stood watch, a sentinel, letting the space transform and be the place it always was. As long as we had the ground, and as long as we kept him company, we were not homeless, which was Carl's definition of tragedy.[10]

It is the image of Carl standing sentinel, marking territory, waiting for the Yellow House to emerge out of the ruins of Katrina, that speaks to the longing for family, for home. In this case, despite Carl's best efforts, the house never emerges from the rubble, and Carl cannot restore the imagined past he so desperately clings to.

You do not have to experience a major trauma in life like Sarah Broom or Natasha Trethewey to long for what has been lost to you. Writing about what you long for helps you understand what you *value*. Perhaps you had an illness or accident as a young child and you felt isolated from your friends and neighbors. Perhaps one of your parents died when you were a young child and your surviving parent remarried. Perhaps your best friend died unexpectantly. What is it that *you* want to find out by writing about it? How did it mark you? Why do *you* care about this? Asking yourself why you care about some incident in your life is important. The answer will help you feel entitled to tell your own story.

RECONCILIATION WITH THE ABSENT FATHER

The archetypal pattern of loss and grief depicted in the ancient Homeric *Hymn to Demeter* is described in memoirs not only about the loss of mother and home but also about the loss of the father. In *The Duke of Deception*, the memoirist Geoffrey Wolff finds himself on a son's quest—after his father has died—to discover who his father, a con man, really was. His father, Duke, lied about everything to everyone: his background, his education, his service as a fighter pilot in the Royal Air Force in England, his war record. Everything about him seemed outsized. Wolff compared him to an encyclopedia image of the Easter Islanders' huge sculptures—massive head and nose. When Wolff tells a friend that he is writing about his father, his friend responds,

> In writing about a father, one clambers up a slippery mountain, carrying the balls of another in a bloody sack, and whether to eat them or worship them or bury them decently is never cleanly decided.[11]

His friend refers here to one of the oldest Greek myths about the gods in which Uranus, the ruler of the universe, is overthrown by his son Cronus, who was jealous of his power. Cronus castrates his father with a sickle given to him by his mother, Gaia, and casts his testicles into the sea. Blood spills out of Uranus and falls to the earth as his testicles fall into the waves. Cronus then learns from Gaia that he too is destined to be overthrown by his own sons, just as he had overthrown his father.

As his children are born—Demeter, Hestia, Hera, Hades, and Poseidon—Cronus swallows them. When his wife, Rhea, gives birth to their sixth child, Zeus, she tricks Cronus by handing him a stone wrapped in swaddling clothes and hides Zeus away on Crete. Cronus swallows the stone, thinking it is his son, Zeus. When Zeus grows up, he overthrows his father by tricking him to disgorge his siblings. Zeus eventually becomes the supreme ruler of all the deities. Wolff, too, tries to disgorge his father by uncovering his lies:

> I wish my father had done more headlong, more elegant inventing. I believe he would respect my wish, be willing to speak with me seriously about it, find some nobility in it. But now he is dead, and he had been dead two weeks when they found him. And in his tiny flat at the edge of the Pacific they found no address book, no batch of letters held with a rubber band, no photograph. Not a thing to suggest that he had ever known another human being.[12]

And yet in writing his memoir, Wolff discovers he is a writer because he is the son of his father, an inveterate liar. He has been left behind to tell his father's story.

> One day, writing about my father with no want of astonishment and love, it came to me that I am his creature as well as his get. I cannot now shake this conviction, that I was trained as his instrument of perpetuation, put here to put him into the record. And that my father knew this, calculated it to a degree.[13]

Centuries apart, both the mythic Telemachus and the memoirist Wolff search for the absent, elusive, inaccessible father in a desire for connection. Telemachus and Wolff idealized their fathers as boys and had to dispel the idealization in order to come to terms with their fathers as men. Unless a son discovers who his father is, he will not know who or what he is. We are endlessly curious about our forebears and how we are made in their image. Dani Shapiro is right: we cannot escape the tangled roots of our ancestors—thick, rich, and dark—that bind us to the earth.

FAMILY SECRETS

In *The Woman Warrior: Memoirs of a Girlhood Among Ghosts*, Maxine Hong Kingston asks the reader what the difference is between a myth and a family story. Twenty years before writing her remarkable book, Hong Kingston's mother told her a story about an aunt in her village in China who had committed suicide. "You must not tell anyone," said her mother. "What I am about to tell you. In China your father had a sister who killed herself. She jumped into the family well. We say that your father has all brothers because it is as if she had never been born."[14]

The aunt, her father's sister, had gotten pregnant out of wedlock and was ostracized by the villagers for breaking cultural norms. They were afraid that the spirits would punish them for her defiance of the village structure.

On the night her baby was to be born, the villagers attacked the family home. They threw mud and rocks at the house, slaughtered their livestock, broke into the house, destroyed bowls, and took sugar and oranges to bless themselves. The aunt gave birth in the pigsty that night, and the next morning she and the baby were found dead in the family well.

"Don't let your father know that I told you" Hong Kingston's mother said. "He denies her. Now that you have started to menstruate, what happened to her could happen to you. Don't humiliate us. You wouldn't like to be forgotten as if you had never been born."[15]

But Hong Kingston never knew whether her mother's "talk stories"—in this case, a warning about sex—were true or myths to instruct her about life as a first-generation American. "Whenever she had to warn us about life, my mother told stories that ran like this one, a story to grow up on. She tested our strength to establish realities. Those in the emigrant generations who could not reassert brute survival died young and far from home."[16]

> My aunt haunts me—her ghost drawn to me because now, after fifty years of neglect, I alone devote pages of paper to her, though not origamied into houses and clothes. I do not think she always means me well. I am telling on her, and she was a spite suicide, drowning herself in the drinking water. The Chinese are always very frightened of the drowned one, whose weeping ghost, wet hair hanging and skin bloated, waits silently by the water to pull down a substitute.[17]

The ghost of her aunt continued to haunt her and she wondered about her obligation to her. "I have thought that my family, having settled among immigrants who had also been their neighbors in the ancestral land, needed to clean their name, and a wrong word would incite the kinspeople even here. But there is more to this silence: they want me to participate in her punishment. And I have."[18]

In writing about her aunt, Hong Kingston breaks silence. She dares to have a voice in spite of her mother's warning. Breaking silence is the driving force behind many memoirs. There is always conflict when other people don't want you to reveal a family secret. Hong Kingston writes her aunt back into life because she knows that her real punishment was not the raid inflicted by the villagers but the family's deliberate forgetting of her. She refuses to participate in that erasure.

WRITING BELIEVABLE CHARACTERS

In writing memoir, we need to make ourselves and
others into believable characters our readers can recognize. Identify the little details about your characters
that make them stand apart from the crowd. You don't
know what they think, so you have to rely on what
they say or do, their mannerisms and dialogue. Sarah
M. Broom writes about her brother Carl standing
watch as a *sentinel* at the remains of the Yellow House,
and we can feel his longing for the place that is gone.
When Toni Morrison writes that the image comes first
and tells her what her memory is about, she is referring
to her recollection of the *sound* of her mother's voice
when she and her friends traded gossip around the
kitchen table about a particular woman in their small
town. The *tone* of her mother's voice changed. It carried a certain "knowing" that informed Morrison that
the woman had broken some taboo and become an
outcast.

In *The Duke of Deception*, Geoffrey Wolff compares
his father to an encyclopedia image of the Easter
Islanders' huge sculptures—massive head and nose—as
a description not only of his physical appearance but
also his psychological impact on others. It is not always
necessary to feel affectionate toward a character, but
it is always necessary to be interested. What does your
character look like? How do you show that?

WRITING PROMPTS

Use one or more of these prompts to inspire your writing:

1. How would you describe your parents or guardians, your grandparents?
2. Wolff uses the metaphor of the massive heads of the Easter Islanders' huge sculptures to describe the psychological size of his father. Is there a metaphor that describes your father?
3. Trethewey uses the metaphor of the yellow narcissi to describe her relationship with her mother. What metaphor or artifact represents your relationship with your mother?
4. What draws you to the stories of your ancestors?
5. What guidance did your mother or father give you? How does it continue to live in you?
6. What is the gift given to you by your forebears? My father gave me the pocket watch given to him by his father, who died before I was born. It had value to me not only as a keepsake but also as representation of the energy of these two creative men.
7. What happens when you hold on to silence?

4

●

WHAT IS MY JOURNEY?

Every day is a journey, and the journey itself is home.
—BASHŌ, *The Narrow Road to the Interior*

THE MYTHIC JOURNEY is taken by a hero or heroine. The journey of the memoirist is taken by an ordinary person but it often follows the same trajectory as the mythic quest. Joseph Campbell delineated the stages of the quest of the mythological hero in *The Hero with a Thousand Faces*.

At its simplest, a mythic journey has three stages: a separation from the known world, trials or challenges, and a return. More specifically, the hero responds to or refuses a call to adventure, crosses the threshold into unknown territory, meets an ally who assists him on his path, and confronts adversaries that try to block his progress. The hero then experiences a series of trials that test his skills and resolve before he can find the treasure or knowledge he seeks. He meets a mysterious partner in the form of a goddess or god, enters into a sacred union, and embarks upon a return trip home. My focus in writing *The Heroine's Journey* was to delineate stages of the journey of the heroine to heal the wounded feminine on a personal and cultural level.

The mythic hero or heroine usually is born under mysterious or unusual circumstances, like the virgin birth in the case of Jesus and the birth of Athena out of her father's head. Marked for greatness by a special sign, the mythic hero, like Zeus, is exiled so that they cannot be killed. Some memoirists, too, are marked with a special sign.

The memoirist Natasha Trethewey writes about being marked from birth on the back of her thigh by a large birthmark that looks like a place on a map, somewhere her mother might have dreamed of going but had never been. In *Memorial Drive* she writes,

> Across cultures myths abound about the imprint a mother can make even before her child crosses the threshold into the world, the way her desires or fears can be manifest on the body. . . . Seeing it is not unlike encountering a forgotten scar, a remnant that recalls the moment of wounding.[1]

Three weeks after her mother is murdered by her stepfather, Trethewey has a dream in which her mother asks the question, "Do you know what it means to have a wound that never heals?" Thirty years later, Trethewey returns to the scene of her mother's death to answer that question and to heal that same wound.

Markings occur in both myths and memoirs. Odysseus is recognized by his old nurse on his return from Troy by the wound on his thigh he suffered as a boy. Trethewey is never really separated from her mother because she bears a birthmark on the back of her thigh, a map that connects the two of them forever.

CROSSING THE THRESHOLD:
THE JOURNEY BEGINS

As I have written in *The Heroine's Journey*, the journey of the feminine begins with an initial separation from the mother that feels like a split from her essential nature. Our archetypal heroine crosses the threshold, meets allies and adversaries in search of an identity in a masculine-defined culture, and faces challenges to overcome certain denigrating cultural myths about women. Finding secular rewards unsatisfying, she goes through an initiation and descent to the goddess to reclaim the depths of her lost feminine soul. Her return journey involves a healing of the initial split from her mother and a reconciliation with masculine aspects of her being. Ultimately the goal of her quest is to find balance in the disparate facets of her nature. Aspects of the heroine's journey—separation, betrayal, abduction, descent, return—also inform the trajectory of many women's memoirs. A fall from grace, a betrayal, a rape can trigger an awareness that life as known before has to change.

And so the journey begins.

In *Crazy Brave*, the Creek poet Joy Harjo writes about her reluctance to cross the threshold to be born because of the generational pain inflicted on her people. She responds to the call, however, because she knows she has gifts to bring her Native American tribe.

Though I was reluctant to be born, I was attracted by the music. I had plans. I was entrusted with carrying voices, song, and stories to grow and release into the world, to be of assistance and inspiration. These were my responsibility. I am not special. It is this way for everyone. We enter into a family story, and then other stories based on tribal clans, on tribal towns and nations, lands, countries, planetary systems, and universes. Yet we each have our own individual soul story to tend. As I approached the doorway to Earth, I was hesitant to enter. I kept looking over my shoulder. I heard the crisp voice of the releaser of souls urge me forward. "Don't look back!"[2]

Harjo heeded the voice of her God and stepped forward. Her memoir is about becoming a poet in the face of obstacles put in her way by her family and her tribe because of her gender. However, she knew that the purpose of her art was to change the conversation for those who came after her, so she continued to believe that her words had value.

BETRAYAL

The Kiss by Kathryn Harrison, perhaps more than any other contemporary memoir, demonstrates the archetype of betrayal. Like the maiden Persephone, Harrison grew up without a father. Having not seen him since she was ten, she was curious about "the hidden parent, the other half of me" and invited him to visit her and her mother for a weekend.[3] The visit was set for spring break of her junior year in college, right after her twentieth birthday. Harrison picked up her father at the airport, and this man, a minister who lived in another state, looked at her as no one had ever looked at her before. She writes that "his hot eyes consume me."[4] When she returns him to the airport after their awkward visit, the betrayal begins.

With his hand under my chin, my father draws my face toward his own. He touches his lips to mine. I stiffen. . . .

As I pull away, feeling the resistance of his hand behind my head, how tightly he holds me to him, the kiss changes. It is no longer a chaste, closed-lipped kiss. My father pushes his tongue deep into my mouth: wet, insistent, exploring, then withdrawn. . . . I am frightened by the kiss. I know it is wrong, and its wrongness is what lets me know, too, that it is a secret.[5]

A father who seduces a daughter enacts a monstrous betrayal not unlike the betrayal of Persephone by her father, Zeus, who condones her abduction by her uncle, his brother Hades. Hades grabs Persephone from the meadow as she reaches out to pick a hundred-blossom narcissus and takes her to the underworld. The kiss in the airport between Harrison and her father begins a passionate affair where they meet in distant cities where no one will recognize them. They continue to meet until Harrison can pull herself out of the underworld, knowing that her very life depends on her exile from her father. She writes,

In years to come, I'll think of the kiss as a kind of trans-forming sting, like that of a scorpion: a narcotic that spreads from my mouth to my brain. The kiss is the point at which I begin, slowly, inexorably, to fall asleep, to surrender volition, to become paralyzed. It's the drug my father administers in order that he might consume me. That I might desire to be consumed.[6]

ABDUCTION

In *Drinking: A Love Story*, the memoirist Caroline Knapp writes about her own abduction, but it is an abduction into the under-world by alcohol. She describes the passionate love affair she had with it and how a literal physical fall when drunk almost destroyed the lives of her close friend's daughters.

> I put the older girl, Elizabeth, on my back, piggyback, and then I picked up the younger one, Julia, and held her facing me, so that her arms were around my neck and her legs around my waist. I was sandwiched between them, holding 130 pounds of kid. Then I started running across the street, shouting like a sportscaster: "It's the Double Marsupial Hold! They've accomplished the Double Marsupial Hold!" And then I lost my balance. This is the truth: I was extremely drunk that night and I put those kids in serious jeopardy.[7]

Three months after this incident, Knapp quit drinking and began the "long slow process of disentangling myself from a deeply passionate, profoundly complex, twenty-year relationship with alcohol."[8] She writes, "Yes: this is a love story. It's about passion, sensual pleasure, deep pulls, lust, fears, yearning hungers. It's about needs so strong they're crippling. It's about saying good-bye to something you can't fathom living without."[9]

Knapp loved the way alcohol made her feel and its ability to shift her focus away from her own emotions. But her father's death, followed a year later by her mother's death, landed her in rehab. As her father had once told her, "Losing a parent is a life-altering event."[10] He knew that his death would have the power to force certain changes in Knapp's life. She describes her descent as having the feeling of "a swan dive, a long, slow, curving arc, the outlines of which I was able to see only in retrospect."[11]

Having the courage to take that swan dive allowed Knapp to make new choices and put them into words.

DESCENT

When Cheryl Strayed was twenty-two, her mother died and then her marriage ended, her family scattered, she struggled with addiction, and her life fell apart. She, too, was in a descent. Four years later and still grieving the death of her mother, Strayed decided to hike the 1,100-mile Pacific Crest Trail from the Mojave Desert through California and Oregon to Washington State in an attempt to put her life back together. Before she left for her solo hike, she marked herself by getting a tattoo of her mother's favorite horse inked on her arm. In *Wild: From Lost to Found on the Pacific Crest Trail*, she writes about how the tattoo was a metaphor of her relationship with her mother:

> I set up my tent, crawled inside, and zipped myself into my sleeping bag, though now I wasn't even remotely tired, energized by the eviction and the late-night hike.
> . . . I smoothed my hands over my arms, hugging myself. I could feel my tattoo beneath my right fingers; could still trace the horse's outline. The woman who'd inked it had told me that it would stand up on my flesh for a few weeks, but it had remained that way even after a few months, as if the horse were embossed rather than inked into my skin. It wasn't just a horse, that tattoo. It was Lady—the horse my mother had asked the doctor at the Mayo Clinic if she could ride when he's told her she was going to die.[12]

For *Strayed*, the heroine's journey is both physical and deeply emotional. She actually walks the stages of the journey: separation from the feminine, bone-chilling grief, descent, and return through a healing of the original mother-daughter split. Inked with the tattoo of Lady, her mother accompanies her on her journey.

In *Let's Take the Long Way Home*, the Pulitzer Prize–winning author Gail Caldwell writes about her own descent into grief as a result of the death of her dearest friend, Caroline. She uses the metaphor of their daily walks—a journey—around a reservoir in Boston to write her memoir about their friendship and her inevitable loss.

> My life had made so much sense alongside hers: For years we had played the easy daily game of catch that intimates connection implies. One ball, two gloves, equal joy in the throw and the return. Now I was in the field without her; one glove, no game. Grief is what tells you who you are alone.[13]

Caldwell's attachment to Caroline reminds me of the friendship between the mythic twins Castor and Pollux, who are portrayed as inseparable best friends. When Castor is killed on one of their adventures, Pollux begs his father, Zeus, to allow him to die with his friend so that they can always be together. Zeus is so touched by Pollux's love for Castor that he gives him a choice. He can go with Castor or share his immortality so that they alternate between the gods in Olympus and the mortals in the underworld. Pollux chooses to be with Castor so Zeus places them together in the Gemini constellation where their fixed positions guide sailors on their travels. Limited by the fact of her mortality, Caldwell is not accorded the same relief.

Know My Name by Chanel Miller demonstrates the courage
it takes to pull oneself out of a descent. Raped by a Stanford
student, Miller describes a culture biased to protect perpetra-
tors, indicting a criminal justice system designed to fail the
most vulnerable. Her memoir exposes the trauma experienced
by victims not only as a result of sexual assaults but also what
happens when the victim refuses to remain silent. Miller forces
the reader to look at the way she was treated by the criminal
justice system.

In the following passage, she is on the stand testifying
about being sexually assaulted. Her assailant's defense attorney continually interrupts her testimony to undermine her.
She finally can no longer take the constant interruptions. She
writes,

I let go, emptying my lungs into the grape-sized micro-
phone. Guttural sounds crawled out of my throat, long
and loud. I didn't collect myself, didn't take my little sip
of water, didn't daintily dab at the tips of my eyes, didn't
say I'm okay, just decided you will wait for as long as it
takes. . . .

I realized this was it, rock bottom, I was touching the
bottom. It could not get any worse. . . . Everything I feared
would happen happened, was happening. Now there was
nothing to do but slowly crawl back out.[14]

Women memoirists—as well as racial, ethnic, and gender-
nonconforming minorities—are told to stay small, remain
silent, not take up too much space; to be likable, to know our
place. We are told that nobody wants to read a memoir by an

angry woman, particularly an angry woman of color. Silencing is a massive hurdle to be overcome, and Miller overcomes it when she testified that, no, she did not give her assailant permission to rape her and, no, she was not the one at fault.

Think about the times you have silenced your own writing because of the fear that others will judge you. The truth is that you, like Miller, will be judged if you put your truth on the page. You will be told, "You can't do that." You will be told that you will lose friends, family members, jobs if you write about what is important for you to write. Miller wanted others to learn from her trauma, and through her writing she was able to change her relationship to what happened, not only for herself but also for her readers. It's through sharing hard truths that we claim our experience and connect with our reader.

After her assailant was convicted, Miller found there was a whole army of invisible survivors behind her. While she was feeling alone, women all over the country were following her case.

Yet all along there had been eyes watching me, rooting for me, from their own bedrooms, cars, stairwells, and apartments, all of us shielded inside our pain, our fear, our anonymity. I was surrounded by survivors, I was part of a *we*.[15]

Each of these women memoirists writes about aspects of her journey—Harjo wills herself to cross the threshold into poetry, Harrison confronts betrayal by her father by writing about it, Knapp survives an abduction into addiction, Strayed and Caldwell tread through the grief of loss, and Miller finds out that she was never really alone. Each woman found the courage to write about her journey so that others might feel empowered to follow. There is a universality to memoirs. Yes, our personal story is important because we write not only for ourselves but also for the others whose lives reflect our experiences and feelings. As Miller wrote, "I was surrounded by survivors. I was part of a we."

CRAFTING YOUR MEMOIR

VULNERABILITY IS AUTHENTICITY

When you are writing about yourself, you are writing about all of us to a certain degree. The struggle for emotional truth is central to memoir. The reader must trust that you have done a fair amount of introspection and that you're trying to give us your best understanding of a particular memory. If you stay at the same flat level of self-disclosure and understanding throughout, the piece may be smooth but will not awaken a sense of self-recognition from within the reader.

The reader cannot expect you, as writer, to remember every single detail or conversation accurately. But the reader has the right to expect that what you claim to be true will be accurate to the best of your recollection. Be careful not to describe yourself and the people in your memoir as fixed, one-dimensional characters. If you write your truth, your reader will care about you and the people in your life as well. Your writing will appear authentic, which is much more important than making you look good.

The memoirists in this chapter, particularly Caroline Knapp and Chanel Miller, were willing to expose their vulnerability to show the reader what it takes to be authentic. There will always be a chance of memoirists being criticized for being too angry, too vulnerable, too revealing, too sad. Women, in particular, are told to stay small, not to take up too much space. Society expects people to be likable, nice, straight, white, able-bodied, and mentally sane. It's understandable that we'd be afraid of making people unhappy or angry at us. We're afraid that our life will be available for everyone to see and that people will judge our life rather than our writing. So we end up judging ourselves. But we can't escape judgment, because judgment is inherent in writing memoir. It takes courage to write your truth.

WRITING PROMPTS

YOUR LIFE JOURNEY

Use one or more of these prompts to inspire your own writing:

1. What obstacles have you faced along your journey? How did you overcome them?
2. Have you ever felt betrayed by a loved one? How did that experience make you feel?
3. What did you learn about yourself from dealing with adversaries in your life?
4. Describe a time when you, like Caroline Knapp, hit rock bottom.
5. What sacrifice did you make along your way?

6. Chanel Miller found that there were invisible allies all over the country supporting her. Who have been the allies in your life?
7. Have you ever been silenced? How did you overcome being silenced?

5

WHAT IS MY PURPOSE?

> The longing to tell one's story and the process of
> telling is symbolically a gesture of longing to recover
> the past in such a way that one experiences both a
> sense of reunion and a sense of release.
> —BELL HOOKS, *Remembered Rapture*

MOST OF US spend our lifetime trying to tease meaning out
of the circumstances of our lives. We search for meaning as we
tell the story about how and where we grew up, who our parents were, how the significant people in our lives influenced
us, what challenges and obstacles we faced, and how we dealt
with triumph and failure. The story we tell ourselves and others gives us a sense of identity. It helps us organize our life in a
way that gives it meaning and direction.

Gender, culture, economic background, religious beliefs,
sexual identity, class, and age all inform our personal mythology and memoirs. We are living through a time when all the
stories the larger culture tells us about ourselves are being
rewritten: what it means to be a man or a woman, what it
means to be a child, what it means to love oneself or other
people. In a time when cultural myths about women and men

are being challenged on every front and there is a political and religious impetus to return to scripts of the past, many people are searching for a deeper understanding of their own story. We write memoir to understand our purpose, why we are here, and how we fit into the greater scheme of things. Such memoirs address themes of vocation, death and rebirth, and remembrance of self.

CALLED TO A CREATIVE LIFE

In *Crazy Brave*, Joy Harjo writes about knowing she was called to become a poet to tell the stories of her people, the Mvskoke (Creek) Nation in Oklahoma. "I was entrusted with carrying voices, songs, and stories to grow and release into the world, to be of assistance and inspiration . . . we each have our own individual soul story to tend."[1] Perhaps she did not know at the beginning of her journey what her "soul story" would be. But as a young single mother, she became aware of what she had to sacrifice in order to become who she was called to be.

> I became the healer, I became the patient, and I became the poem. I became aware of an opening within me. In a fast, narrow crack of perception, I knew this is what I was put here to do: I must become the poem, the music, and the dancer. I would not truly understand how for a long, long time. This was when I began to write poetry.[2]

If you recall the hero's stages of mythological journey from chapter 3, the first stage is responding to the call or refusing the call. Harjo answered the call when she became aware of an opening within herself. She knew her life would be hard—she was kicked out of her family by her stepfather and later she would leave her husband—but she also knew she was called to cross the threshold by the spirit of poetry.

> It was the spirit of poetry who reached out and found me as I stood there at the doorway between panic and love. There are many such doorways in our lives. Some are small and hidden in the ordinary. Others are gaping and obvious, like the car wreck we walk away from, meeting someone and falling in love, or an earthquake followed by a tsunami. When we walk through them to the other side, everything changes.[3]

Myra Shapiro is another memoirist who was called to be a poet in midlife after fulfilling what she saw as her obligation to her husband and daughters. Shapiro writes about her deep desire to live the life of a poet and the journey she takes as she turns fifty to fulfill that desire. Like Harjo, she was *called* to be a poet. *Four Sublets: Becoming a Poet in New York* is her love story about poetry, the poetic life, and becoming a writer in New York City. It is the tale of a spirited woman in midlife who has raised two daughters in Chattanooga and now yearns to create the life of a poet that she longed for as a wife and mother.

Returning home from a trip to Manhattan after her youngest daughter has left for college, Shapiro tries to explain to her husband her desire to live the life of a poet in New York. She declares that at this point in her life, she will let nothing—not even him—stop her from her desire to make art.

> I explained I wanted a community of poets for the writing I'd begun to do, that writing had become more important to me than teaching, and I believed it was my true work, the way I wanted to grow old. "Oh no," he yelled, "if you

do this, don't ever come back." Only with the words I'd learned in the previous ten years from Betty Friedan and Gloria Steinem and the women with whom I'd gathered in consciousness-raising circles could I know what my mother would never have known to say: "You decide what you need to do, but you cannot tell me what I can do. This is my house as well as yours, and I can return to it when I want." Then I added, "I refuse to say years from now *If only . . .*"[4]

Shapiro declares her separation from the particular roles of mother, wife, teacher in midlife. Such a separation from the known world is not always as clearly and passionately articulated. Because of her determination, Shapiro makes a full return to the city of her birth, New York, to give voice to her creative soul.

Certainly not everyone has such a clear sense of their purpose as Harjo or Shapiro, but some memoirists, such as Mary Jane Nealon, know what they *want* it to be from the very beginning. In the opening pages of *Beautiful Unbroken*, Nealon writes, "As far back as I can remember I wanted to be a nurse or a saint. I wanted to be heroic."[5]

Saints were so familiar to me as a child they were like first cousins. I liked to kneel on the brown cushions in the pews and to take communion. I wanted to be a saint. I made a little altar on the marble table in my room and waited for my visitation, but sin was around every corner. I found myself telling little lies; they piled up. Was this the kind of girl who gets visited by an apparition? I had the desire sometimes to faint and just lie on the cold floor of the church while the parishioners walked over me.[6]

Nealon writes that she wanted to be like the Algonquin saint Kateri Tekakwitha, who cared for her fellow Indians suffering from smallpox, or Clara Barton, the founder of the American Red Cross. She wanted to save people. She watched her Aunt Frances, a nurse, walk around their Jersey City neighborhood in her crisp white nurse uniform, taking care of her neighbors' wounds and giving out cough syrup. Nealon decided then that rather than a saint, she would become a nurse.

> It was in this neighborhood that once I started to see the
> impossibility of sainthood, the impossibility of reconciling
> my little thefts and disobediences with the miraculous,
> I paid more attention to my aunt. . . . Among the other
> occasional fantasies I nurtured, like being an astronaut,
> being a nurse took over. I started, innocently enough, to
> begin my entire life.[7]

Beautiful Unbroken is the story of Nealon's life as a nurse during the AIDS/HIV crisis in New York. Nealon's childhood calling to be a saint took form in her work as a nurse during one of the worst epidemics that occurred in the United States in the 1980s. What we are "called" to be is many times out of our hands. And we don't always respond with all of what we are— we are asleep, deaf, avoidant, fearful, self-involved. But we are called to accept our desire and learn what a gift it is to live an ordinary life and to honor our instinctual yearnings.

FINDING ONE'S ROOTS

The writer, composer, and musician James McBride grew up in the Red Hook housing projects in Brooklyn. He was the youngest of twelve Black children in a family with a white mother.

When he asked her why she wasn't the same color as everyone else in the family, she said she was light-skinned. But that wasn't enough for him. He wondered if he, too, was different, and he asked his mother if he was white or Black. When she told him to "mind your own business. Educate yourself or you'll be a nobody!" he decided to find out why they were the only family in the neighborhood with a white mother.

As an adult, McBride set out to learn his mother's origins, which he documents in *The Color of Water*. Over eight years, he wore down her resistance to being interviewed by him. He discovered that she had been born in Poland, raised in the South as the daughter of a rabbi, fled to Harlem where she married a Black man, was disowned by her family, and, as a single mother, put twelve children through college. As McBride uncovered his mother's story using interviews and research, he reclaimed his own identity as a half-Black, half-Jewish man raised by a mother who looked nothing like him.

> She opened the door for me but closed it for herself long ago, and for her to crack it open and peek inside was like eating fire. She'd look in and stagger back, blinded as the facts of her own history poured over her like lava. As she revealed the facts of her life I felt helpless, like I was watching her die and be reborn again (yet there was a cleansing element, too), because after years of hiding, she opened up and began to talk about the past, and as she did so, I was the one who wanted to run for cover. . . . Imagine, if you will, five thousand years of Jewish history landing in your lap in the space of months. It sent me tumbling through my own abyss of sorts, trying to salvage what I could of my feelings and emotions, which would be scattered to the winds as she talked.[8]

There is no way for us to know whether Harjo, Shapiro, Nealon, or McBride found their purpose in writing memoir, but I imagine they did. Most writers of memoir do not know what their purpose is when they first set out to recount their memories. Often there is just a longing or a need to record their accomplishments and challenges, or later, to make sense of their lives. When I started to write *Unreliable Truth: On Memoir and Memory*, I had no plan to write about my mother's death. My original plan was to write about the inextricable nature of memory and identity; I was curious about how Alzheimer's had altered my mother's personality. In the weeks before her death, she found a lightness of being and sense of humor that had previously escaped her.

The hospice nurse told me that my mother would not live through the week. I put my hand on my mother's heart and spoke gently into her ear. "It's okay, Mom, you can let go now." Something changed in the room. The air. Her breathing. The light. I don't know what it was, but it was palpable. I kept telling her to move toward the white light, but then the color changed to blue. "Move toward the blue light, Mom. Mother Mary has her arms outstretched to you." . . . My mother's death was one of the most peaceful and profound experiences of my life. . . . I have wondered about my memory of Mother Mary reaching out to her. Did I actually see it or was it my imagination? Since we can't separate imagination from memory, I will never know.[9]

When I ask students why they have chosen to write a memoir, they often respond, "To understand another," "To heal a relationship," "To heal myself," "To find a broader perspective," "To tell a story that must be told," "To undercover some mystery." Dani Shapiro wrote *Inheritance* to discover the identity of her birth father; Natasha Trethewey wrote *Memorial Drive* to understand how her mother's murder defined her *own* life. "I need now to make sense of our history, to understand the tragic course upon which my mother's life was set and the way my own life has been shaped by that legacy."[10] Jeanette Winterson wrote *Why Be Happy When You Could Be Normal* to find her birth mother and to understand how adoption defined the patterns of her life. She explained, "When I began this book, I had no idea how it would turn out. . . . I was writing the past and discovering the future. I did not know how I would feel about finding my mother. I still don't."[11]

In my experience as a teacher and as a writer of memoir, the initial purpose of writing is triggered by an internal summons to get the story down. Sven Birkerts writes, "Memoir begins not with event but with the intuition of meaning—with the mysterious fact that life can sometimes step free from the chaos of contingency and become story."[12] Most memoirs are about something much deeper than what the writer sets out to write.

People are writing stories not only of their lives but about particular places and times in history. The memoirist cannot separate themselves from what was going on in the culture during the time they are writing. Carolyn Butcher, one of my memoir students, has been writing as an Englishwoman born in the decade after the end of World War II whose mother and grandmother were denied important aspects of normal life because of the two world wars. These two generations of women had each lived under incredible pressure and trauma, which in turn affected the mothering of the next generation,

Butcher's generation. Their lives were circumscribed by war, and they missed out on many aspects of normal life. "Education was free only until the age of fourteen," Butcher writes, "and so my mother was working full-time as a secretary in a real estate office even before she had her first period. There was no time to be a teenager or to make any lifestyle choices."

A reading of her birth chart on her fiftieth birthday helped Butcher understand the purpose of her writing at this time in her own life as a mother and grandmother. She is writing "Make Room for Butterflies," a book-length memoir and gave me permission to use this passage:

> I was in my Chiron return when I had my birth chart
> analyzed by an experienced astrological consultant around
> the time of my 50th birthday. In excellent health, but
> with a family history of death before aged 75, I thought
> an astrological reading might be a stepping-stone to begin
> exploring what I would like to do with the rest of my
> life. Although no specific questions were fully formed in
> my mind that day, looking back I can see my quest was
> elemental in a way Glenda Jackson once explained. In an
> interview she gave when she was playing King Lear, Jack-
> son said the reason Shakespeare's plays remain relevant
> centuries after they were first performed is because they
> ask the three fundamental questions of mankind: *Who am
> I? What am I? Why am I?*
>
> In the years since receiving the reading of my birth
> chart I have mostly forgotten about it, but I am beginning
> to understand that, of the three questions of mankind
> that Glenda Jackson highlighted, it is the *Why am I?* that
> has been worming its way through my skull for some time.
> Today, looking over what the transcript of the birth chart

reveals I see something that shifts my clarity in exploring my narrative question, *What did I come into this world to mend in my family* . . . According to my astrologer, the interesting part of my chart shows that in my growing-up years with my mother and grandmother my emotional needs were invisible. The astrologer said, "There was a deep wounding with your mother which started before you were born, in the embryo."[13]

Butcher had an intuition that it was important for her to write about her mother's and grandmother's lives but had not consciously known how the generational trauma they experienced during wartime had affected her life as well. As the Sven Birkerts quote mentioned earlier states, "Memoir begins not with event but with the intuition of meaning."[14]

FACING THE SHADOW

In his memoir *The Night of the Gun*, the *New York Times* investigative journalist David Carr inquires into his addiction, recovery, and the mercurial nature of memory. He relied on hundreds of medical files, legal documents, journals, and interviews with sixty friends and family members to make his story "as true as I could make it." Many memoirists read old journals, look at photo albums, listen to music, and watch old movies to jog their memories. Carr was unusual in also interviewing scores of people from his past to confirm his memory.

Among others, he interviewed Donald, his best friend from college who was with him on the "worst day of his life" twenty years earlier. That day, Carr lost his job after refusing his boss's offer to go into rehab. Instead, he went on a destructive bender that ended with someone trying to break into Donald's house at gunpoint. After Carr recounted his memory of that night, Donald interrupted him and told him that things did not happen quite the way he remembered.

> We hadn't seen each other in years, but what knit us together—an abiding bond hatched in reckless glory—was in the room with us. I told him the story about the Night of the Gun. He listened carefully and patiently, taking an occasional swig out of a whiskey bottle and laughing at the funny parts. He said it was all true, except the part about the gun. "I never owned a gun," he said. "I think *you* might have had it."[15]

Carr is stunned. He declares that he is not a gun guy because he has been on the wrong end of the barrel of a gun a few times, squirming and sweating and asking people to calm down. He could not imagine himself walking over to his best friend's house and trying to break in with a gun jammed into his pants.

> No chance. That did not fit my story, the one about the white boy who took a self-guided tour of some of life's less savory hobbies before becoming an upright citizen. Being the guy who waved a gun around made me a crook, or worse, a full-on nut ball.[16]

The "guy with a gun" does not match Carr's image of himself. More than anything, he does not want to swallow the reality that he was the guy with a gun. Someone else must have had the gun. He writes,

> Even if I had amazing recall, and I don't, recollection is often just self-fashioning. Some of it is reflexive, designed

to bury truths that cannot be swallowed, but other "memories" are just redemption myths writ small. Personal narrative is not simply opening up a vein and letting the blood flow toward anyone willing to stare. The historical self is created to keep dissonance at bay and render the subject palatable in the present."[17]

Yes, it takes courage to write the selves we may have consigned to shadow. We don't want others to see what we don't want to see in ourselves. The story Carr told himself did not include a guy who was out of control with a firearm. The story Dani Shapiro told herself did not allow for the possibility that she had been conceived with sperm not of her Jewish father but with the sperm of a pale, blue-eyed Christian medical student. Writing memoir gives us the opportunity to explore the answer to the right question—if we are willing.

Shapiro traces her desire to keep dissonance at bay to early comments she had received about her appearance. She had been told throughout her childhood that she didn't "look Jewish" because she was a pale, blond, blue-eyed delicate girl and her forebears were Eastern European dark-skinned Ashkenazi Jews. She was so sure of her parentage that she dismissed any evidence to the contrary—until her DNA proved what she couldn't allow herself to begin to consider.

How was it that I had never suspected? Not even after my mother had let slip the method of my conception? . . . It seems a sliver of doubt would have wedged itself within me. But there was no doubt. No suspicion. I staunchly ignored the evidence. Instead, I sat, glib and certain under the starry Vermont sky, incurious about why this kept happening. *Story of my life* was what I usually said with a shrug and a sigh. A phrase that seemed to cost me nothing. *Story of my life.*[18]

Every mythic quest harbors a question or is motivated by a central question, like the one Butcher began to understand as she wrote her memoir: "What did I come into this world to mend in my family?"

In the legend of the Holy Grail, Parsifal failed to ask the right question. He was a youth who knew nothing of the world, not even of his own origins, and went on a quest to become a knight of the Round Table. He ventured into the Grail castle where he saw the Fisher King with a wound in his genitals or thigh, a wound that would not heal. The king needed a young innocent such as Parsifal to see that something was wrong, have compassion, and ask, "What ails thee?" Only then would the healing qualities of the Grail become available to the king and the kingdom would be united.

Parsifal failed to ask the question. Years later, having engaged in many adventures and reached a turning point in his spiritual education, Parsifal returned to the Grail castle. Seeing the old king's suffering, he asked, "What ails thee?" and the king was healed. It took maturity, wisdom, and compassion to bring forth the healing question.

Every memoir should also have a narrative question that is answered by the end of the book. In *Let's Take the Long Journey Home*, Gail Caldwell finds that the death of her friend, Caroline, didn't end the story of their friendship. "It's taken years for me to understand that dying doesn't end the story; it transforms it."[19]

Sometimes I think that the pain is what yields the solution. Grief and memory create their own narrative: This is the shining truth at the heart of Freud and Neruda and every war story ever told. The death mandates and gives rise to the story for the same reason that ancient tribes used to bury flowers with their dead. We tell the story to get them back, to capture the traces of footfalls through the snow.[20]

Caldwell is correct. Dying doesn't end the story. The heart breaks open with the pain of loss yet the story lives on.

Each one of these memoirists had a purpose in writing their memoir: Joy Harjo and Myra Shapiro answered the call to be poets; James McBride longed to understand his African American and Jewish roots; David Carr wanted to reclaim his memory of a time in his life forgotten; Carolyn Butcher uncovered postwar multigenerational trauma; and Gail Caldwell searched for a way to come to terms with her best friend's death. We write these stories to guide and comfort us, as Caldwell so eloquently states, to "capture the traces of footfalls through the snow."

CRAFTING YOUR MEMOIR

DISCOVERING YOUR WRITING'S PURPOSE

When I ask new writers why they want to write memoir, they have many answers: self-discovery, to understand a relationship, to heal themselves, to find a broader perspective, to understand the trajectory of their lives, to satisfy some mystery they want to discover, to express their grief, and simply to tell a story that must be told. Angela, a student in my memoir class in San Francisco, when writing about a difficult relationship with her father, discovered that the man who had raised her was not actually her birth father. She had always wondered why she felt such awkwardness with her father. When she confronted her mother in her forties, she finally learned the truth. It turned out that her "uncle" who came to visit only on holidays was actually her birth father. Her mother had become pregnant as a very young teenager, and her strict Mexican American family chose an older cousin to marry her. Angela's memoir then became a story of deep compassion for her father and ultimately for her mother as well.

As I wrote earlier, most writers of memoir do not know what their purpose is when they first set out to recount their memories. The very act of writing becomes a journey of discovery. As Glenda Jackson once explained about the relevance of Shakespeare's plays centuries after they were written: "They ask the three fundamental questions of mankind: *Who am I? What am I? Why am I?*" In writing her memoir, Carolyn Butcher discovered that the question she most wanted to answer is "What did I come into this world to mend in my family?" Writing memoir gives us a sense of satisfaction and release. The feminist writer bell hooks writes, "The longing to tell one's story and the process of telling is symbolically a gesture of longing to recover the past in such a way that one experiences both a sense of reunion and a sense of release."[21]

WRITING PROMPTS

Use one or more of these prompts to inspire your writing:

1. Mary Jane Nealon knew she was called to be a nurse at an early age. How and where were you called? How did you feel?
2. What decision did you make as a result of this calling?
3. What pattern in your life began as a result of this call?
4. James McBride wanted to explore his roots as a half-Jewish, half-Black man. What do you want to find out about your roots?
5. Like Carolyn Butcher, is there something you came into this world to mend in your family?
6. What is the Big Truth you feel you can't write about?
7. What narrative question does your memoir seek to answer?

PART TWO

EXPLORING YOUR
ARCHETYPAL THEMES

6

•

WOUNDING AND
THE BODY

Our ragged wounds allow the body to speak its
language.
—DENNIS PATRICK SLATTERY, *The Wounded Body*

THE PSYCHOLOGIST Rollo May suggests that the remembered origin of the wounds we receive in life may be the genesis of our personal myth. In *The Wounded Body*, the distinguished professor of mythological studies Dennis Patrick Slattery writes that the wound is the trace of the memory, what one has left of the experience: "If the body is always an emblem of our history, then its wounded markings are the permanent witnesses to that same body's identity."[1] For example, Odysseus is recognized by his old nurse, Eurycleia, by the scar he carries on his thigh, a mark he received from a boar hunt in his youth. The scar marks his identity, what he has left of the experience.

Prometheus, fire stealer from the gods, is bound to a rock for all eternity, punished with a daily wound. Each morning an eagle perches on his hip and rips out his liver; each night the wound heals, only to be torn open the next day. In stealing fire from the gods, Prometheus's wound becomes his gift for humankind. In Aeschylus's *Prometheus Bound*, Prometheus not only brought fire to mortals but also gave them arts and sciences, as well as the means to survive.

Each one of us has wounds—physical or emotional—that are significant and can inform our memoir writing. My memoir student Peggy G., one of the first women litigators in Los Angeles in the 1970s, recently consulted a psychiatrist for a possible new medication for her ADHD (attention deficit hyperactivity disorder). She had been agitated by her scattered energy, lack of focus, thirst for achievement, and insatiable drive and wanted a new solution. Adderall and other medications she had been prescribed over time made her nervous and shaky. The psychiatrist wisely told her that slowing down and enjoying this phase of her life was not a pathological condition requiring medication. Peggy decided to explore the positive aspects of ADHD, which she calls her "Superpower," in writing.

> ADHD had actually been a powerful tool for me over the decades, when all of life was a competition I had to win. It worked as I juggled four kids and a solo trial practice, crafting cross-examination questions for both kids and clients while I swam 100 laps in our backyard pool every day at dawn. Some of my best work was done underwater.

Writing about the evolution of her ADHD was a revelation to her. Her perception of it as a pathological condition changed, and she began to appreciate how her "wound" had ultimately served her and her family.

Jean-Dominique Bauby, the editor in chief of *Elle* magazine, suffered a massive stroke in his early forties that left him completely paralyzed, a victim of "locked-in syndrome." Locked-in syndrome is caused by damage to the brain stem, leaving the person with a condition in which they have almost complete inability to move any part of their body. Yet they are fully conscious and aware of their surroundings. In Bauby's case, he could blink his left eyelid. His memoir *The Diving Bell and the Butterfly* is a celebration of the liberating power of consciousness even as his body, like that of Prometheus, becomes a prison he cannot escape. "I can listen to the butterflies that flutter inside my head. To hear them one must be calm and pay close attention, for their wingbeats are barely audible."[2]

Bauby writes his memoir in the hospital where he is confined by painstakingly "dictating" each word, letter by letter, to a colleague with the blink of his left eye, the only part of his body he can move.

> My heels hurt, my head weighs a ton, and something like a giant invisible diving bell holds my whole body prisoner. My room emerges slowly from the gloom (of the morning). I linger over every item: photos of loved ones, my children's drawings, posters, the little tin cyclist sent by a friend the day before the Paris-Roubaix bike race, and the IV pole hanging over the bed where I have been confined these past six months, like a hermit crab dug into his rock . . . Paralyzed from head to toe, the patient, (me) his mind intact, is imprisoned inside his own body, unable to speak or move. In my case, blinking my left eyelid is my only means of communication.[3]

After a year of being encased in his lifeless body, Bauby welcomes a season of renewal, knowing that he will never get out of the hospital alive. He watches the activity of the hospital, the assortment of familiar faces he sees daily: the man who brings the linens, the dentist, the mail carrier, and a nurse who has just had a grandson. He comments that this, the start of his first autumn season at the hospital, has made one thing very plain: "I have indeed begun a new life, and that life is here, in this bed, that wheelchair, and those corridors. Nowhere else."[4]

As vulnerable as he is—his world reduced only to what he can hear and what he can see with his left eye—Bauby invites the reader to be present to the world around him and to share with him his wonder at being alive. Dennis Patrick Slattery explains, "Wounds suggest to us that where we are most vulnerable is the place and time which must be most venerated, for they mark a sacred space in us that we would have ignored had not the wound brought it forcefully into consciousness."[5] Bauby's memoir does just that. When he writes that his life is "in this bed, that wheelchair, those corridors, and nowhere else," he reminds the reader that wounding becomes sacred when we are willing to release our old story—our old life—to create space for the new story to emerge into time.

There are many myths about wounds and the body. The god-man Asclepius was said to walk with a crippled leg; the Fisher King had a wound that would not heal; Inanna was hung by her sister Ereshkigal on a peg to rot in the underworld. Chiron, the centaur—half man, half horse—is accidentally shot by Heracles with a poisoned arrow tipped in the Hydra's blood. Because he is immortal and cannot die, he must live forever in agony. But Chiron asks Zeus to remove his immortality so he can die from his wound. Chiron becomes the "wounded healer," using the pain of his wound to heal others. His wound becomes its own salve. Those, like Bauby, who have confronted the reality of death through accident or illness often return to life with a renewed sense of wonder and strength. Wounding is the training ground for the healer.

INVISIBLE WOUNDS OF BIRTH

Wounding involves a penetration or opening into the human flesh or soul by a force, power, or energy coming from beyond our ordinary recognized boundaries. Athena is birthed through an opening in her father Zeus's head and forever remains a father's daughter. Jeanette Winterson describes the birth of a child as a wound of its own. "The baby's rupture into the world tears the mother's body and leaves the child's tiny skull still soft and open. The child is a healing and a cut."[6] For Winterson, adoption is a wound as well. It is the genesis of Winterson's personal myth that something is always missing—and that something is mother.

> Adopted children are self-invented because we have to be; there is an absence, a void, a question mark at the very beginning of our lives. A crucial part of our story is gone, and violently, like a bomb in the womb.
>
> The baby explodes into an unknown world that is only knowable through some kind of a story—of course that is how we all live, it's the narrative of our lives, but adoption drops you into the story after it has started. It's like reading a book with the first few pages missing. It's like arriving after curtain up. The feeling that something is missing never, ever leaves you—and it can't, and it shouldn't, because something is missing.[7]

This particular wound may be invisible, but Winterson feels marked by it for life. Her story cannot be separated from her longing for what has been lost.

WOUNDS WE DO NOT SEE

There are the wounds that society doesn't see and there are wounds that society doesn't *want* to see. Chanel Miller wrote *Know My Name* to reclaim her identity after surviving a brutal sexual assault by Brock Turner, a Stanford University student. Using her name as well as the name of her assailant in her memoir was her attempt to transform the hurt inside herself, to confront an assault the university did not want to be accountable for, and to find a way to live with and incorporate her memories.

> I always wondered why survivors understood other survivors so well. . . . Perhaps it is not the particulars of the assault itself that we have in common but the moment after; the first time you are left alone. Something slipping out of you. Where did I go. What was taken. It is terror swallowed inside silence. An unclipping from the world where up was up and down was down. This moment is not pain, not hysteria, not crying. It is your insides turning to cold stones. It is utter confusion paired with knowing.[8]

The betrayal of women by powerful men has been recounted in endless myths, but none as poignant as the ancient Greek Agamemnon's betrayal of his daughter Iphigenia. He deceives her by summoning her to Aulis, where the Greek ships await their siege of Troy, with the promise of marriage to the noble warrior Achilles. She arrives with her mother, Clytemnestra, to prepare for her marriage and soon discovers that Agamemnon plans to sacrifice her to the gods in exchange for a wind to blow the Greek ships to Troy. Agamemnon begs his daughter's understanding and his wife's forgiveness, saying, "This is a fearful thing, yet I must do it. Unless this sacrifice is made, the seer swears we can never reach Troy: and all the Greeks are burning to smite the foe. If Paris goes unpunished for the theft of Helen, they believe that the Trojans will come to Greece and steal more women—steal their wives—steal you and our daughters."[9]

Agamemnon excuses the murder of his daughter by professing to have no alternative. He chooses his love of war and country over the value of his daughter's life just as Miller is asked to keep her experience to herself to preserve the reputation of the potential Olympic swimming champion who is her assailant. In both instances the women are wounded by cultural misogyny. Miller writes,

> When I get worked up over what happened, I tell myself, you are a pair of eyes. I'm a civilian who's been randomly selected to receive an all-access pass to the court system. . . . My job is to observe, feel, document, report. . . . I write to show how victims are treated at this moment in time, to record the temperature of our culture.[10]

Chanel Miller is scarred by the experience of not only being raped by her assailant but also being brutalized by the criminal justice system that further wounds victims. Her assailant was convicted of three counts of felony sexual assault but sentenced to only six months in jail because the judge felt that a "lengthier sentence would have a severe impact on his life"; never mind her life. Even though Miller has no visible scar to show, she carries the imprint of the trauma, which serves as a distinct reminder of the injuries to her body and psyche.

RESILIENCE FROM WOUNDING

Jeannette Walls begins her memoir *The Glass Castle* with her earliest memory of being on fire. At age three, she was standing on a chair in her pink tutu in front of the stove in the family's trailer in southern Arizona cooking a hot dog by herself. Her tutu caught on fire. The burns covered her entire body, and the doctors at the hospital told her she barely survived. They took patches of her skin from her upper thigh and put them over the burned parts of her stomach, ribs, and chest. When they were finished, they wrapped her in bandages. Walls writes,

> Look, I'm a half-mummy, I said to one of the nurses. She smiled and put my right arm in a sling and attached it to the headboard so I couldn't move it. The nurses and doctors kept asking me questions: How did you get burned? Have your parents ever hurt you? Why do you have all these bruises and cuts? My parents never hurt me, I said. I got the cuts and bruises playing outside and burns from cooking hot dogs. They asked what I was doing cooking hot dogs by myself at the age of three. It was easy, I said. You just put the hot dogs in the water and boil them. . . . Two nurses looked at each other, and one of them wrote something down on a clipboard. I asked what was wrong. Nothing, they said, nothing.[11]

At age three, Walls had already learned to make light of a perilous physical situation. *The Glass Castle* is an extraordinary memoir about resilience. Jeannette and her siblings learned to take care of themselves as children—feeding, clothing, and protecting each other from a father who drank too much and a mother who was deeply dysfunctional. The children eventually made their way to New York where Jeannette became a journalist. Their parents followed, choosing to remain homeless even as Jeannette and her siblings tried to house them. Walls's body became the narrative marked by the scars of her experiences.

WOUNDING OF MOTHER AND MOTHER EARTH

The wounds we carry are mirrored by Mother Earth. In the spring of 1983, the poet and Mormon environmentalist Terry Tempest Williams, found out that her mother was dying of cancer. That same spring, the Great Salt Lake began to rise to record heights, threatening the Bear River Migratory Bird Refuge with its myriad of birds—gulls, herons, snowy egrets— whose count began to decrease. Her memoir *Refuge* describes her struggle to come to terms with both her mother's cancer and eventual death as well as the wounds to the body of Mother Earth inflicted by fallout from nuclear tests in Nevada. She writes as a member of what she calls "The Clan of One-Breasted Women":

> My mother, my grandmothers, and six aunts have all had
> mastectomies. Seven are dead. The two who survive have
> just completed rounds of chemotherapy and radiation.
> I've had my own problems: two biopsies for breast cancer
> and a small tumor between my ribs diagnosed as "border-
> line malignancy." . . . Most statistics tell us breast cancer
> is genetic, hereditary, with rising percentages attached to

fatty diets, childlessness, or becoming pregnant after thirty. What they don't say is living in Utah may be the greatest hazard of all.[12]

As her mother's cancer progresses, Williams is challenged to find a new perspective on life and accept the way her mother chooses to deal with her upcoming death. Her mother says, "Just let me live so I can die. Terry, to keep hoping for life in the midst of letting go is to rob me of the moment I am in."[13] Williams endures through her connection with nature; she cannot save her mother just as she cannot save the birds of the Great Salt Lake.

> Last night I dreamed I was walking along the shores of the Great Salt Lake. I noticed a purple bird floating in the waters, the waves rocking it gently. I entered the lake with cupped hands, picked up the bird and returned it to shore. The purple bird turned gold, dropped its tail, and began digging a burrow in the white sand, where it retreated and sealed itself inside with salt. . . . In the next segment of the dream, I was in a doctor's office. He said, "You have cancer in your blood and you have nine months to heal yourself."[14]

Her mother begs Williams not to overidentify with her illness. She can't stop her mother from dying, but she can learn to love the time she has left with her. "If I can learn to love death then I can begin to find refuge in change."[15] Ultimately she finds solace in the realization that the cancer process is not unlike her own creative process.

> Ideas emerge slowly, quietly, invisibly at first. They are most often abnormal thoughts, thoughts that disrupt the

quotidian, the accustomed. They divide and multiply, becoming invasive. With time, they congeal, consolidate, and make themselves conscious. An idea surfaces and demands total attention. I take it from my body and give it away.[16]

The Native American writer Sherman Alexie is another poet who learns to shake off the wound of grief through his connection to nature. He wasn't present on the reservation when his mother, Lillian, died. But soon after her death, a small brown bird flew into his kitchen window, knocking itself out, and crashing to his deck. Alexie considered putting it out of its misery, but then the bird began to regain consciousness and raised one wing to the sky. It shook that wing and then raised its other wing and shook it to the sky as well. The little bird shook and shook both its wings and then stood up.

Alexie, who had had a very complex and difficult relationship with his mother, felt pain about not having been with her when she died. In *You Don't Have to Say You Love Me*, Alexie writes that he sat with his therapist a few weeks after his mother's funeral and told her the story of the small brown bird's pacing and shaking. His therapist told him that she was a birder and loves birds.

And when they hit a window like that, or get hurt in any significant way, they have this ritual. They shake off the pain. They shake off the trauma. And they walk in circles to reconnect their brain and body and soul. When your bird was walking and shaking, it was remembering and relearning how to be a bird. . . . We humans often lose touch with our bodies. We forget that we can also shake away our pain and trauma.[17]

Jean-Dominique Bauby teaches us that wounding can lead to consciousness; the invisible wound of adoption scars Jeanette Winterson for life; both Chanel Miller and Jeannette Walls rise resilient surviving their wounds; and Terry Tempest Williams and Sherman Alexie are both gifted with the image of birds that reframe the wounds of their loss. Being wounded reminds us that we are human.

CRAFTING YOUR MEMOIR

USING SENSORY DETAILS

Scenes, vignettes, episodes, slices of reality are the building blocks of memoir. The uninspired writer will *tell* the reader about a subject, place, or personality, but the memoir writer will *show* that subject, place, or personality in action.

The memoirist Mary Karr writes that in crafting a scene, the writer must help the reader experience smell, taste, touch, image, and sound.[18] The more sensory you can make your scene, the easier it is for your reader to enter it with you. When writing a scene, choose a detail that is memorable. Describe the setting where the scene takes place and a time frame for the action. Necessary elements for scenes include place, time, action, problem, characters, and sensual details.

Jeannette Walls begins *The Glass Castle* telling the reader that she is a three-year-old standing on a chair alone in front of the stove in the family's trailer (place, time, character). She is wearing a pink dress her grandmother has given her. Pink is her favorite color. She writes, "The dress's skirt stuck out like a tutu, and I liked to spin around in front of the mirror thinking I looked like a ballerina" (sensory detail). Yet in this particular moment, while she stands on the chair, she is cooking hot dogs watching them "swell and bob in the boiling water" (detail). Her tutu catches on fire, and she ends up with burns covering her entire body (action).[19]

Walls has crafted a scene in such a way that the reader will never forget her as a three-year-old wearing a pink tutu, cooking hot dogs. She has written these details so distinctly that the reader can feel what she is experiencing. In writing memoir, think about what you want your reader to get out of the scene. What do you want them to know or understand?

___

WRITING PROMPTS

YOUR BODY AND WOUNDS

Use one or more of these prompts to inspire your writing:

1. How and where were you wounded? How did it feel?
2. What does your body remember?
3. How has your body been marked?
4. Odysseus is recognized by the scar he carries on his thigh. It marks his identity. Do you have a scar that marks your identity?
5. What story does your body yearn to tell?
6. What is trying to be born in you from that wounding?

7. Chanel Miller writes about the personal and cultural wounds we do not see. Have you participated in ignoring those wounds?

7

•

HOME AND
HOMECOMING

I had lost not only a place but the past that goes with
it and, with it, the clues from which to construct a
present self.

—EAVAN BOLAND, *Object Lessons*

IN *THE BOOK OF SYMBOLS* Ami Ronnberg explains, "In
mythologies all over the world our first home is a paradise
of oneness, a time before consciousness and its conflicting
discriminations . . . the goal of epic odysseys, spiritual quests
and psychic transformations."[1] Hestia was the Greek goddess
of the hearth, the center of the home, the center of the earth,
our own personal center. In the Greece of antiquity, the house
was built around the hearth, and Hestia *was* the hearth. Hestia was concerned with bringing together those who formed
a household. She protected the family and sheltered it from
discord. The temple of Hestia served the same function for the
town. Quarrels and fights could not take place in front of Hestia because the hearth was a place of peace and security. The

hearth was sacred. If Hestia's fire went out in the home or in the town, there were complex rituals to relight it.[2]

The archetype of home is at the heart of our collective longing. How do we define home? Is it a structure, a place, or is it the beloveds who embody the structure? Terry Tempest Williams writes, "Each of us finds our identity within the communities we call home."[3]

For Odysseus to return home to Ithaca, he needs first to remember who he is by recounting the narrative of his twenty-year-long journey to the Phaeacians. Sarah M. Broom addresses what happens when a family's home is destroyed by a natural disaster like Hurricane Katrina, shattering the hearth, scattering the family. And the Pulitzer Prize–winning journalist Jose Antonio Vargas writes that if you are undocumented in America, there is no home.

In *Dakota*, the award-winning poet Kathleen Norris returns to her ancestral home in the Great Plains after living in New York City and writes that "desert wisdom allows you to be at home, wherever you are."[4] The British novelist, playwright, and poet Deborah Levy writes about what happens when we get the home we have dreamed of and yet our psyche is still not soothed. "It was as if the search for home was the point, and now that I had acquired it and the chase was over, there were no more branches to put in the fire."[5]

In *Don't Let's Go to the Dogs Tonight*, Alexandra Fuller, who grew up in Rhodesia (present-day Zambia), found that when she left home as an adult, her roots were too embedded in Africa for her soul to find peace anywhere else. And the actor Gabriel Byrne dreams of the home in Ireland he left at age ten, only to find that like life, it has been irrevocably changed. In *Walking with Ghosts*, he writes,

How many times have I returned in my dreams to this hill. It is always summer as I look out over the gold and green fields, ditches foaming with hawthorn and lilac, river glinting under the sun like a blade. When I was young, I found sanctuary here and the memory of it deep in my soul ever after has brought me comfort. Once I believed it would never change, but that was before I came to know that all things must. It's a car park now, a sightseer's panorama.[6]

When Byrne recounts the hill of his dreams, he is, perhaps unknowingly, describing a longing for the sanctuary of home. The archetype of home is what we long for the most. I am struck by the courage of the migrants at the southern border who gather together daily around the fire (their own cultural fire), finding community, finding sanctuary, longing to find home. Think of the home you have lost or longed for as you read the narratives that follow.

HOME OF BELONGING

Memories of home can release a life story. The memoirists in this chapter write to find out who they are, where they have come from, and where they are going. As they reflect on their narratives about home, they begin to understand how home structures their identity.

Jana Zimmer, one of my memoir students, was born in Prague after World War II but raised in Montreal. Yet she longs for the home of her imagination. She imagines that if she had never left Prague as a baby, her psyche would have felt at home. Her sense of smell brings back her memories. In *Chocolates from Tangier* she writes,

This notion of home continues to baffle me. I am home in Prague when I smell lilacs, or eat sauerkraut with bread dumplings, or Oblatentorte, and when I am staying with my soul sister, Simona, in Podolí. I am home in Montreal, also, when I smell lilacs, or eat smoked meat on rye, or pea soup. And on my only visit to Jerusalem- where I do not speak the language, cannot even read the street signs, and feel no kinship with the modern Israeli, I marched myself through the labyrinths of the Old City and I stood crying at the Western Wall- the non-Jews call it the Wailing Wall. But my roots are not at the bottom of a well, there. Or are they? I have always romanticized this notion of home and belonging. I want a place and a people who would wholeheartedly welcome me and take care of me. I have never had that and now I think that I never will, at least not as I imagined it.[7]

As an archetypal theme, the hunger to *belong* embraces all aspects of life. Joan Didion writes, "A place belongs forever to whoever claims it hardest, remembers it most obsessively, wrenches it from itself, shapes it, renders it, loves it so radically that he remakes it in his own image."[8] For Didion, that was Los Angeles; for Zimmer, the place that has claimed her is Prague. For the American critic and memoirist Vivian Gornick, it is New York City where she walks every day to absorb the drama, humor, and humanity of the streets. In *The Odd Woman and the City*, Gornick writes,

Each day when I leave the house, I tell myself I'm going to walk up the East Side of town because the East Side is calmer, cleaner, more spacious. Yet I seem always to find myself on the crowded, filthy, volatile West Side. On the West Side life feels positively thematic. All the intelligence trapped inside all those smarts. It reminds me of why I walk. Why everyone walks.[9]

Gornick is invigorated with every section of the city she calls home, where she runs into friends and talks to strangers. Born in the city, she cannot abide living anywhere else. She runs into her friend Victor, an unhappy dentist with a Caesar haircut and sad brown eyes, who has lived in her neighborhood for years. Standing there together on Fourteenth Street, a Con Ed drill blasting in their ears, Victor croons to her:

> "Dahling, sweetness, beautiful girl, how *are* you, still living in the same building?"
> "Yes," I reply.
> "Still doing journalistic work?"
> "No, Victor, I teach now."
> He pushes his chin out at me as though to say, "Tell me."
> I tell him. He listens intently as the words fall rapidly from my mouth, nodding steadily as I speak of the deprivation of spirit I suffer living for months at a time in one university town or another.
> "It's exile!" I cry at last. "Exile pure and simple."[10]

He knows exactly what she means. "Victor and I are now quarantined on this island of noise, spellbound by matters of the soul."[11] Gornick finds her identity in the community she calls home.

WHAT REMAINS WHEN HOME IS LOST?

Sarah M. Broom writes about the Yellow House that was destroyed by the winds and rains of Hurricane Katrina and what that house symbolized for her. "My mother was, I can see now, the house that was safe. But still, we carried the weight of the actual house around in our bodies."[12] She discovers that everyone has an opinion about what to do with the house. "There was the house we lived in and the house we thought we should live in. There was the house we thought we should live in and the house other people thought we lived in. These houses were colliding."[13] When the house fell down, something in Broom opened up. "Houses provide a frame that bears us up. Without that physical structure, we are the house that bears itself up. I was now the house."[14]

Even after the house is destroyed, Broom cannot erase it from her mind. She tries to live in different cities on the West Coast and the East, but she keeps coming back to New Orleans, unable to find home. "I wanted to be free from its lock and chain of memory, but did not, could not, foresee water bumrushing it. I still imagined, standing there, that it would one day be rebuilt."[15] After the house is demolished, her brother Carl continues to go to the empty lot to drink beer with his buddies as if the house is still there.

Broom eventually writes a letter to the house, asking it to let her go: "It is obvious that you are gone and yet you are not. Our psyches keep you. You are ravenous and gluttonous."[16] Like a magnet, the house of what Toni Morrison calls her "re-memory" keeps drawing Broom back. In her epic novel *Beloved*, Morrison writes, "If a house burn down it's gone, but the place—the picture of it—stays, and not just in my re-memory, but out there in the world. What I remember is a picture floating around out there outside my head."[17] It is Broom's "re-memory" that haunts her and won't let go.

Many of us may long to fit into our past selves, but most of us are only somewhat comfortable in our former homes. It is our imagination of what was in the past that holds us. The award-winning author Kathryn Schulz writes, "Even if we love them, even if we sometimes long for them, even if we know them down to the last ancient orange spatula in the kitchen utensil drawer, we inevitably outgrow them."[18] Yet they still play a large part in our imagination. Gabriel Byrne writes,

> It was winter, New York. I was an exile emigrant and immigrant, belonging everywhere and nowhere at all. Home is where the heart is but the heart itself had no home. . . . As a child I would escape hurt and loneliness by taking refuge in stories I would create for myself. Later as an adult when I found my identity shattered by sorrow or even success, when I didn't know who I was, I retreated into a world of imagining.[19]

Byrne found home in the stories he creates. Another immigrant, Jose Antonio Vargas, retreated into a world of compartmentalization and writes about what it means to not have a home.

LIVING AT THE MARGINS

Jose Antonio Vargas left the Philippines at age twelve to live with grandparents in California. He didn't learn until he was sixteen that the "uncle" with whom he had flown to the United States was a smuggler and that the green card and passport his grandfather provided for him were fake. He learned then that he couldn't get a driver's license, a social security card, accept certain jobs, or travel out of the country because he wasn't a citizen. One of over eleven million undocumented immigrants, he had to organize his life in such a way that no one knew who he really was. He wanted to be a journalist and needed to pass as an American citizen so that he could work, and yet he had to remain invisible so he didn't draw too much attention to himself. His relationship with people was shaped with secrets and lies; he spent "years if not decades passing in some kind of purgatory."[20] Despite becoming an award-winning journalist, Vargas never felt at home. In *Dear America: Notes of an Undocumented Citizen*, he writes,

Since I began writing, the three most dangerous words in the English language for me have been "I," "me," and "my." That's partly because I've internalized the axiom that I need to "earn" my American citizenship that I'm uncertain if I'ved "earned" the right to express myself in such personal terms. It's also partly because I'm afraid of what happens when I confront my own despair, the sense of disorientation and abanadonment I've been grappling with since arriving in this country as a motherless twelve-year-old. I run away from people, especially people who want to get close. I run away from myself. Because I've never felt at home, because I've never had a real home, I've organized my life so I'm constantly on the move and on the go, existing everywhere and nowhere. I live at airports, which is somewhat fitting, since my life was changed that one morning in an airport in a country I left to go to a country where I've built a life that I have not been able to leave.[21]

Journalism was a way of separating what I do from who I am, a way of justifying my compromised, unlawful existence to myself: *My name may be at the top of this story, I may have done all the reporting and the writing, but I'm not even supposed to be here, so I'm not really here.*[22]

Vargas founded the nonprofit organization Define American to change how immigrants are seen with the hope of changing the politics of immigration. He was detained in McAllen, a border town in Texas, when he tried to report on the children who were detained at the border. It was while sitting in a jail cell with the young boys who had crossed the border that he realized that like them, he was truly homeless. He didn't belong in the Philippines, the country of his birth, nor in the United States, which was his home but wasn't. "It's dangerous out there, and home should be the place we we feel safe and at peace. Home is not something I should have to earn. Humanity is not some box I should have to check."[23]

Because he was a famous reporter, he was ultimately released from detention after friends called their contacts at the Department of Homeland Security and the White House. But after twenty-five years of "passing" in the United States, Vargas decided he no longer wanted to hide from the government or hide from himself. It was time to go home.

HOMESICKNESS

The artist Susan E. King writes about being homesick for Kentucky, the land of her birth, during the years she lived and worked in California, the land of her youthful longing. Like Zimmer, King yearns for the home of her birth and feels exiled when away from it. She writes, "I'm always homesick even though I travel a lot. The distance really doesn't matter." In *Redressing the Sixties*, King writes,

> While in California, I spent decades thinking and writing about Kentucky and childhood. I felt embarrassed by my subject matter. As if I had a choice. Then I read about

James Joyce living in Paris and writing *Ulysses*. About how he'd query his Dublin friends about street names in Dublin when they visited him in Paris. About how he studied Dublin phone books. And I began to understand my longing. I learned about many of the European refugees that had landed in Los Angeles before and during WWII. Scores of writers, such as Thomas Mann, actors, directors, artists and composers. My immigration to California wasn't being played out on the world stage, although California was attracting my generation in the 1970s. It was as far as most of us could move west and still be in the U.S. Where, as Joan Didion wrote: "things better work here, because here, beneath the immense bleached sky, is where we run out of continent." I'd moved about as far from Kentucky as I could.[24]

While teaching a workshop for artists in Australia once, she blurted out that she was homesick. She had just bought a house in Kentucky and felt ripped away from it by teaching halfway around the world.

BARREN HOME: THE EMPTY NEST

The British writer Deborah Levy avoids thinking about the end of motherhood and facing an empty nest as her youngest leaves for university by creating a blurred image of home. In *Real Estate*, she constructs an imaginary home by collecting objects to which she becomes attached, like a banana tree she buys in her London market. Her daughter teases her, calling it her "third child," and asks, "How is your new child doing?" as she points to the tree.[25] Like many women facing an empty nest after the rigors of motherhood, the idea of "home" is a longing and a loss. Levy writes:

I was also searching for a house in which I could live and work and make a world at my own pace, but even in my imagination this home was blurred, undefined, not real, or not realistic, or lacked realism. I yearned for a grand old house (I had now added an oval fireplace to its architecture) and a pomegranate tree in the garden. It had fountains and wells, remarkable circular stairways, mosaic floors, traces of the rituals of all who had lived there before me. That is to say the house was lively, it had enjoyed a life. It was a loving house.[26]

Now that the end of her "epic motherhood" was moving her into a new phase of life, Levy imagines a grand old house—not an empty nest but a house that has weathered the vagaries of life where she, too, can populate it with life and loving. She contends with the passage of time and what it means to be a woman and an artist after mothering by stretching her imagination wide with dreams of grandeur.

LONGING FOR HOME

Like King, I have a chronic case of homesickness, and the ache for home feels ancestral to me. For years I had the same recurring dream: a whitewashed thatched roof cottage on a gentle incline, a woman in a light-blue dress sitting in a rocking chair in front of the hearth, a black iron kettle hanging over the fire. She stares out the window at a body of water. She is waiting for someone to return from the sea.

During my first visit to Ireland in 1975, I kept looking for the thatched cottage of my dreams. Certainly there were many of them on the Aran Isles, in Kerry and Dingle, but I couldn't find *my* cottage. It felt like it was located northwest, somewhere near Clifden, near the sea. In 1990 I returned to Ireland with my daughter, Heather, and her friend, Holly, and told them about my dream. We stayed in Clifden for several days, but I saw no cottage that felt familiar. The day we left Clifden to return east to Newgrange, Holly pestered me to find my cottage.

"We can't leave until we find it," she insisted.

Surprised and pleased that she was willing to entertain my dream, I took a back road out of Clifden. About five miles after we had left the main road, I took an abrupt right up a small narrow lane where there was an old, abandoned, graying whitewashed cottage sitting in the middle of the bog. It didn't have a thatched roof; the tin roof was rusting, but it called to me.

Paying more attention to the cottage than the road, I drove the car into a ditch and couldn't get it out. As we walked around the car looking for a way to extract it from the mud, a man in a battered brown station wagon came down the lane and told us the nearest tow truck was at the gas station back in Clifden. I thanked him and stared at the ruin of the cottage that stood on a slight incline up the lane from the ditch.

"Let's go check it out," said Holly. "Maybe it's your cottage."

"No," I said, "it can't be. There's no water around here."

"Let's go anyway," the two girls said excitedly, "before we have to hike back into town to get a tow."

We trudged across the mucky bog, sinking into the mud, and crossed the threshold into the house. It was clear the cottage had not been occupied in decades. It was in complete disrepair; there was no door, no glass in the windows, and the walls were cracked. The room we entered had a hearth on the right, the remains of an iron pot hanging from a hook. I walked to the hearth and the hairs at the back of my neck began to tingle.

"Come here and look what I found," called Holly. I went into a small adjoining room, which perhaps had been a bedroom, to find Holly looking out the open space where a window had once been. There in the distance was water. Not the sea but a body of water we had not seen from the road.

Carl G. Jung, Sigmund Freud, and other psychoanalytic theorists believed that individuals are destined to act out apocalyptic themes of ancient history that are handed down from generation to generation through not only the institutions of society but in the collective unconscious. The Irish are great dreamers and value fantasy, the unseen realms, and the wisdom of the land. It was no "accident" that I drove into the ditch that day; the cottage of my dreams wanted to be found.

At the core of the Irish American story is the longing for home and the unresolved questions related to loss, place, and identity. Although I am four generations removed from those of my relatives who fled Ireland in 1846, I still long for that elusive metaphor—home. Like the Irish poet Eavan Boland whose epigraph began this chapter, I wonder if I will ever unearth the clues from which to construct a present self.

CRAFTING YOUR MEMOIR

STORY OVER STRUCTURE

When you start writing memoir, don't worry about structure. Let your memories and images lead you. You won't know what your structure is until you've written your memories. Too many writers stop writing because they think they have to know their structure as they begin to write. Memoir does not work that way. There are no set guidelines for structuring a book-length memoir, although I know that Claire Fontaine and Mia Fontaine, the authors of *Come Back: A Mother's and Daughter's Journey through Hell and Back*, used the technique of storyboarding to structure their memoir. But that was because they were screenwriters.

You can have a liner narrative in chapters, telling your story from beginning to end as in *Angela's Ashes* by Frank McCourt or *Eat, Pray, Love* by Elizabeth Gilbert. Linear memoirs are often coming-of-age stories.

Or you can start at the end of your story and then jump back to the beginning, like Jeannette Walls does in *The Glass Castle*; or weave the story back and forth through time, like *Pieces of My Mother* by Melissa Cistaro. In Cistaro's book, each chapter alternates between two time frames: Then, when she was a five-year-old child and her mother left the family; and Now, as she is an adult and her mother is dying. Claire and Mia Fontaine also alternate chapters in *Come Back*, with each chapter reflecting their different voices as mother and teenage daughter.

Joan Didion keeps circling back to the opening scene when her husband dies in *The Year of Magical Thinking*, and Cheryl Strayed focuses on an eighteen-month period of her life as she hikes the Pacific Coast Trail. She weaves in backstory about her mother's horse and reflects on it but always returns to the "present" of her trek on the trail.

In *The Liar's Club*, Mary Karr keeps coming back to a pivotal interaction with her mother from the opening page of the book but does not let the reader know what happened—and what it meant—until the end of the book. In *The Duke of Deception*, Geoffrey Wolff uses the frame of his father's death at the beginning and end of the book and devotes the middle of the book to finding out who his father was.

Some memoirists are more focused on theme, concept, or idea rather than timeline and explore the nature of their subject in depth. For example, Caroline Knapp's writing focuses on her alcoholism in her memoir *Drinking: A Love Story* and Dani Shapiro explores the issue of paternity in *Inheritance*.

More and more writers are experimenting with different forms in writing memoir. The memoirist and teacher Abigail Thomas writes short chapters about a particular era in her life in *Safekeeping*, and Sherman Alexie combines prose and poetry in *You Don't Have to Say You Love Me*. The Afghan writer Homeira Qaderi writes *Dancing in the Mosque* as a letter to her son.

Reading other memoirs will inspire you and might give you an idea about how to structure yours. In the meantime, write!

WRITING PROMPTS

YOUR HOME

Use one of more of these prompts to inspire your writing:

1. What does an image of home evoke for you?
2. How do you define home? Is it a place, a person, a landscape, a feeling in your body?
3. Describe a dream about home.
4. What remains when home is lost?
5. Have you ever felt like you didn't have a true home? Describe that sensation. Where did it lead you?
6. Where have you found your greatest sense of home?
7. How do you come home to yourself?

8

•

EXILE AND BELONGING

As soon as you leave your place of belonging, in a
strange way, you don't belong anywhere else.
—GABRIEL BYRNE, *Walking with Ghosts*

OUR VERY EXISTENCE begins in exile. We come into life
having already been exiled—physically, most intimately from
our mother's womb and archetypally from the Garden of Eden
by our foremother Eve. When Eve plucked the apple from the
tree of the knowledge of good and evil, our ability to endlessly
float in the warm amniotic sea of the unconscious came to an
end. Because of Eve's curiosity, she and Adam were banished
from the Garden of Eden when exile, which is an early motif
in ancient Greek tragedy, was seen as a fate worse than death.

Lilith, known as the first Eve, exiled *herself* from the Garden of Eden because she refused to submit to Adam and lie
beneath him in sexual intercourse. She based her protest and
claim for equality on the fact that each of them had been created by God from the clay of the earth. When she saw that
Adam would overpower her, she uttered the ineffable name of

God and flew up into the air, eventually living in a desert cave on the shores of the Red Sea.

In the Hebrew book of Exodus, exile meant establishing an "exodus paradigm," a model for people yearning to escape bondage to reach a "promised land." The book of Exodus tells the story of Israelite enslavement and departure from Egypt. After leading the Israelites out of Egypt and crossing the Red Sea, Moses led them into the Sinai, where they spent forty years wandering in the wilderness. They camped at the foot of Mount Sinai where God appeared to Moses, giving him the Ten Commandments. The Exodus narrative is a founding myth of the Jewish people, providing an ideological foundation for their culture and institutions.

Voluntary exile, like that of the Israelites, is often depicted as a form of protest by those who claim it, to avoid persecution and prosecution. It also occurs as a result of an act of family shame or as a way to isolate oneself to devote time to a particular pursuit. In her memoir *Beautiful Country*, the Chinese American author Qian Julie Wang writes that her father *chose* exile from China because of the shame he felt when his eldest brother was arrested for writing an essay criticizing Mao Zedong, the founder of the People's Republic of China. As a result of his brother's offense, her father, seven years old when his brother was arrested, spent his entire childhood being bullied and berated by classmates for belonging to his "treasonous" family. As an adult, he and his wife emigrated to the United States with their daughter, expecting it to be the promised land, a place of safety and serenity. However, the Wangs found that many who have chosen exile or have been exiled from their home often find themselves living in the shadows.

Qian Julie Wang, who accompanied her parents to the

United States from China as a seven-year-old, writes about living in the shadows of immigration in *Beautiful Country*.

> On July 29, 1994, I arrived at JFK Airport on a visa that would expire much too quickly. Five days prior I had turned seven years old, the same age at which my father had begun his daily wrestle with shame. My parents and I would spend the next five years in the furtive shadows of New York City, pushing past hunger pangs to labor at menial jobs, with no rights, no access to medical care, no hope of legality. The Chinese refer to being undocumented colloquially as "hei": being in the dark, being blacked out. And aptly so, because we spent those years shrouded in darkness while wrestling with hope and dignity.[1]

Wang writes about the shame she experienced, feeling "other," separate, different, and impoverished. She decided to write her memoir for the forgotten children who, like her, grew up fearing that at any moment they could be deported from their new country for being "illegal." Every day her mother reminded her that they were not allowed in the United States. She said, "Don't trust anyone."

"I didn't understand what that meant," writes Wang, "but every time we walked past other Chinese people, I could tell that they didn't trust us, either."[2] Mei Guo (the United States) was not the promised land her family in China had thought it would be, and Wang found it hard to feel safe.

> Everything smelled strange and looked different. We lived in a place that BaBa [Father] called Brooklyn. Most of the people around us had brown skin and dark hair. Other than our Cantonese landlady, we rarely ever saw anybody

who looked like us, and when we did, they never talked to us in Chinese. I wondered if we had left behind the only place in the world that had our people.[3]

Every night, Wang looked at her reflection in the shared bathroom of their apartment house, poking at her cheeks and tugging at her eyelids to see if she had a flat "pancake face" like a Chinese colleague of her father's. She didn't look different to herself but wondered why white strangers called her a "Chink," a word her father said was bad. Almost every day someone said it to her and her mother as they walked down the street, reminding her she didn't belong. She also developed ways to make herself invulnerable. "I learned quickly that people were dangerous. But I also learned that there were certain expressions, of anger and coldness, that I could wear to keep people a little farther away. I started to put on a mask of those expressions every time I left home."[4] It is no wonder why she felt that she didn't belong.

GENERATIONAL TRAUMA

Najla Said, the daughter of a Lebanese mother and famous Palestinian father, was born in the United States and raised in the Upper West Side of Manhattan. She writes about the effect of exile on the next generation and, like Wang, her experience of being "othered." Because of her Arabic roots, she never felt like she belonged in a Jewish neighborhood in New York that she grew up in. As a child and adolescent, she felt like her face was wrong, her brown "cow-eyes" were wrong, her body was wrong, and even though she was baptized Episcopalian and was not a Muslim, she didn't want to be associated with "dirty" Arabs. She even starved herself to a state of anorexia.

Whenever her friends' parents asked her where her parents were from, she would deny their heritage. She felt weird, ugly, dirty and acted out in the Waspy private middle school she attended. It wasn't until the end of high school that she began to feel a sense of belonging.

After she graduated from high school, Said's parents took her and her older brother back to Palestine. It was the first time her father, Edward Said, had returned to the land of his birth since being exiled in 1947.

> Daddy and his immediate family were not actually forced out of the house by Israelis in 1948, but rather had left in 1947 and taken up permanent residence in their second home, in Cairo. But though the family was lucky enough to not see their village burned, their town renamed, and their passports rendered useless; though they didn't end up in a refugee camp in Palestine, Jordan, or Lebanon, with only an identity card and no basic rights, nonetheless, their home was taken, along with all of their possessions, and they were exiled, never to be allowed back as anything but visitors. And the privilege of being a visitor was bestowed on them thanks only to the American citizenship my grandfather had passed on to them as a result of the many years he had spent in the States.[5]

As the family walked the narrow streets of the Old City of Jerusalem, Najla looked for people who looked like her. Like Wang, she searched the faces of others to find *her* people. In *Looking for Palestine*, she writes,

> I would constantly look around to find a face that understood me, that recognized me as someone who belonged

there. I found comfort nowhere but in the faces of the Palestinian children we met along the way. They, like me, were silent. They very clearly had no control over their surroundings. They were simply born into this history, and just like me, they had no memories of a Palestine other than the one in which they lived. . . . They were victims of the circumstances of their birth in a way that I would never be.[6]

Said realized that the Israeli children she saw in Palestine also bore the burden of their ancestors. "None of us had emigrated or immigrated or fought in wars or suffered the Holocaust, but we still were the ones who had to bear the burdens of our peoples' respective histories."[7] The science of epigenetics holds that traumatic events our forebears endured can implant a "tag" onto the genes in our DNA. The information on the "tag" is passed down along with the gene, carrying with it psychological and behavioral experiences of the parent or grandparent.[8] I imagine that Said's inability to feel that she belonged anywhere could reflect not only her own experience but the experience of her exiled father as well.

In *Water Thicker Than Blood*, George Uba agrees that the trauma experienced by his Japanese parents, who were interned in American camps after the Imperial Japanese Navy Air Service bombed Pearl Harbor, left an indelible mark on him even before he was born.

It always starts before you are born. Always starts with preceding generations, their hardships, perils, traumas, which in your early years you believe are simply yours to hear about, to collect in fragments, to wonder at, to sympathize with, until gradually you realize that your life connects to that past in ways you had not foreseen. . . . I thought my life began in Chicago. I was mistaken. That is where my body first made its appearance, but the contours of my life, just like the contours of my brother's and sister's lives, had their start much sooner.[9]

In his memoir, Uba describes the intergenerational trauma he was subjected to as a result of the suffering his Japanese parents and grandparents experienced interned in the tar-paper barracks of the camps. The past may be gone, but it is still alive in the DNA of succeeding generations. Like children of individuals who survived the Holocaust, Uba experienced personal indignities and invisible scars left from his ancestors who had been wrenched from their homes, friends, and businesses, and from the hopes and plans for succeeding generations.

DOES ANYONE LOOK LIKE ME?

Those who emigrate to a new land often end up subconsciously searching to find someone who looks like them in their new environment. They peer at the color of a stranger's eyes, the shape of their eyes, the color of their hair. Both Qian Julie Wang and Najla Said write about looking for a face that will confirm that they belong. In *The Mask of Oyá*, Flor Fernandez Barrios, who fled Castro's Cuba with her family when she was fifteen, writes about how her skin color, hair color, eye color, and height set her apart from the teenagers in her new country.

In the years following my arrival in America, I was less than proud to be Cuban. I call that time the dark phase of my development, when I would have gladly exchanged

my dark hazel eyes for a pair of blue ones. As a fifteen-
year-old, I was plagued by a desire to turn my black hair
into blonde. Dyeing my hair would not have disguised
my origins because, unlike many of my Hispanic friends
who were lucky enough to have a fair complexion, I had
skin that was brown. The innocent but intrusive inquiry,
"Where are you from?" made me feel separate and different from the rest of the White world. . . . No matter how
hard I tried to disguise my ethnicity, my heavy accent was
stubborn and defiant.[10]

As a little girl in Cuba, Barrios had been close to her grandmother, Patricia, who taught her the rituals and healing herbs
of a curandera, a healer. Arriving in the United States, Barrios tried to forget the teachings of the spirit world in order
to assimilate with American teenagers. Ten years after her
arrival, her grandmother came to visit to remind her of who
she was, no matter how she tried to hide her ethnicity.

In her trip to Los Angeles, she had prepared me with
spiritual tools to bring forth the same healing energy she
had called upon in her practice in Cuba. The context was
different, but what I learned after many years of reflection
was that there was no need for altars and candles. Inside
the modern ambience of my (therapy) office space lived the
world of Oyá with her invisible winds of transformation.[11]

VOCABULARY OF BELONGING

For those who have been forced to leave home, the archetypal
theme of longing for home never really dissipates. The trauma
from leaving is inherited by the next generation and the next.

In *The Family Silver*, the professor of American cultures and professor of English Sharon O'Brien writes that for those who left Ireland during the famine of the 1840s, it's clear that "both those who stayed in Ireland and those who left, never to return to their homeland, were marked emotionally and psychologically, and that inheritance marked their children and grandchildren."[12]

During the Great Hunger (1845–1849), the population of Ireland was reduced from eight million to just five million people, and everywhere there was death, starvation, and forced emigration. It was the worst catastrophe in western Europe in the nineteenth century. Over one million people lay dead in less than five years and two million more emigrated to the US during the next decade. The scale of flight from Ireland in coffin ships to America was unprecedented in the history of international migration. Other groups who left eastern Europe thought of themselves as immigrants, but the Irish considered themselves "exiles," cut off by English landlords from their land and communities.[13] The departure, the leaving, and the sorrow of never going back "home," and the piece of the self that was lost in that forced departure, are still embedded in the Irish American psyche.

The Irish learned to suppress what happened to them. In their determination to put the savage experience of the famine behind them, many survivors denied its relevance, escaping into alcohol and frequently crippled by shame, guilt, and a mortal fear of being exposed as inherently bad or perpetually wrong. This was due to the legacy of colonialism and the Irish Catholic Church's espousal of a theology of fear that led them to believe they had been born bad due to original sin and deserved to suffer. They worked hard to prove their worth. Frank McCourt of *Angela's Ashes* writes,

The Irish were ashamed of themselves when they got here. They dropped the O's and the Mc's from their names. They were so busy hanging on, and then prospering and coming right up against the establishment, they lost sight of themselves.[14]

In *Object Lessons*, the Irish poet Eavan Boland writes that an emigrant and an exile are not necessarily the same thing. There is at least an illusion of choice about being an emigrant, although sooner or later they will share the desolation of feeling exiled. But both need a paradigm. "The expatriate is in search of a country; the exile, like the memoirist, is in search of a self. He or she learns how to look for it in a territory between rhetoric and reality, with its own customs and habits of mind, its preferred speech and rigorous invention."[15]

Boland left Ireland at age five when her father took a job in England. When she returned to the country of her birth at age fourteen, she found that what she called "her vocabulary of belonging" was missing. "The street names, the meeting places—it was not just that I did not know them. It was something more. I had never known them. I had lost not only a place but the past that goes with it and, with it, the clues from which to construct a present self."[16]

She found herself reconstructing a childhood that had never really happened. She used her imagination to construct details of a life lived in Ireland while she was in exile:

I began to watch places with an interest so exact it might have been memory. There was that street corner, with the small newsagent which sold copies of the *Irish Independent* and honeycomb toffee in summer. I could imagine myself there, a child of nine, buying peppermints and walking back down by the canal, the lock brown and splintered as ever, and boys diving from it.[17]

In this way, using her imagination, Boland located herself in an Irish childhood she had longed for "in a territory between rhetoric and reality," creating what she called the "last unwanted gift of exile."[18]

VOLUNTARY EXILE: *READING LOLITA IN TEHRAN*

For two years before she left Iran in 1997, Azar Nafisi gathered seven young women, her previous university students, at her house every week to read and discuss forbidden works of Western literature. They came from various backgrounds: conservative and religious, progressive and secular, and some formerly incarcerated. Over that time, the women began to talk not only about the novels they were reading but also about themselves, their dreams of freedom, and their disappointments. When Nafisi decided to move her family out of the oppression of Iran to the United States, the women felt betrayed by her decision, yet many later decided to follow her example.

> Our decision to leave Iran came about casually—at least that is how it appeared. Such decisions, no matter how momentous, are seldom well planned. Like bad marriages, they are the result of years of resentment and anger suddenly exploding into suicidal resolutions. The idea of departure, like the possibility of divorce, lurked somewhere in our minds, shadowy and sinister, ready to surface at the slightest provocation. If anyone asked, I would recount the usual reasons for our departure: my job and

my feelings as a woman, our children's future and my trips to the U.S. which had once more made us aware of our choices and possibilities.[19]

Once the decision was made, Nafisi deferred packing and refused to talk about her departure seriously. Her attitude made it difficult for her students to know how to respond; she never discussed her decision to leave, and they felt that they couldn't bring it up. It was understood that the class could not continue indefinitely, but Nafisi realized that her decision to leave was a betrayal of some unspoken promise she had made to her students. They were all anxious and sad at the thought of the class ending. "Your place will be so empty, Yassi had said, using a Persian expression—but they too began to nurture their own plans to leave."[20]

Some of her students made it out of Iran to England or Canada where they started new lives. Others stayed and tried to make the best of their lives. Nafisi settled in Maryland and took a teaching position at Johns Hopkins University. In *Reading Lolita in Tehran* she writes, "Going away isn't going to help as much as you think. The memory stays with you, and the stain. It's not something you slough off once you leave."[21]

BELONGING/NOT BELONGING: YOU CAN'T GO HOME AGAIN

Alexandra Fuller returned to Zambia, the country of her girlhood, after she was left feeling shattered by the divorce from her American husband in Wyoming. She returned home in May, her favorite time of year on her parents' farm in Zambia. It was the end of the rainy season before the fires start in the valley. Her father talked to her about selling the family farm and asked if she wanted to return to Zambia permanently to work it. But even though she didn't know what lay ahead, she knew that the farm wasn't the place where she belonged. Southern Africa had changed so much in the twenty years since she had left that it was no longer familiar. In *Leaving Before the Rains Come*, Fuller writes,

Our forests, which had been my deepest memory of Zambia's essence, were vanishing so fast it was like seeing someone in the unstoppable course of a disease. It was likely that elephants and lions would no longer exist in the wild here well within my lifetime.[22]

The rate of loss in the land had estranged her. Like Evan Boland, Fuller found that her vocabulary of belonging was missing. After her father asked her about returning to the farm, they walked back to the camp where her mother, sister, and nieces were playing cards. A fire was burning in the firepit, meat was cooking, and the dogs were curled up at people's feet. It was a comforting scene.

But she had left Africa two decades before with her husband for what she thought of as the Promised Land. They built a home, had children, and established a life there where unfortunately, their two cultures came into opposition. She had changed as much as southern Africa had.

It was deeply comforting and familiar, and yet I knew I no longer really belonged here. At least, I had lost my unequivocal sense of belonging. I'd fledged too hard, flown too urgently from the nest, been carried off by stronger trade winds than I could fight against. And now I was solo, truly. And it was okay.[23]

CULTURAL EXILE

Cultural exile occurs when an individual or group is born into a culture and chooses not to conform to the norms of that culture or is unable to because of a compelling physical or emotional makeup. When a culture does not accept or tolerate a person who is "different" or who refuses to conform, they are "exiled" and forced to live apart, often physically as well as emotionally. Think about individuals who find themselves exiled from their family or their religion because of political beliefs or sexual orientation. Homeira Qaderi writes about being exiled as a woman demanding her rights as a mother in a patriarchal culture.

Qaderi grew up in Afghanistan under Taliban rule, where girls and women have no rights, no opportunity to be educated, and no ability to choose or refuse a spouse. They live under constant fear that any trace of personal rebellion can cost them their lives and the lives of family members. Yet Qaderi rebelled at age thirteen and defied the strictures of a misogynistic social order, risking her freedom by hiding books under her burka to teach reading and writing to children in her native village.

Like Metis, the mother of Athena who was swallowed by her consort, Zeus, to deny her the honor of giving birth, Qaderi experienced a similar erasure of her identity. Prior to 2020, when Qaderi gave birth, an Afghani female was held in such little esteem that her name was not even listed on her child's birth certificate. Qaderi's name was not recorded on the birth certificate of her newborn son, Siawash—only the name of his father and the father's father. Qaderi's grandmother tells her, "In this land, it is better to be a stone than to be a girl." After fifteen years of marriage to a husband she did not choose but had come to love, Qaderi refused to accept her husband's desire to take a second wife, one of his university students. Qaderi rejected the practice of becoming a number—number one wife——and tells him she will not accept it. She has had a taste of freedom by teaching in Kabul, becoming a published author, and learning how to drive, and she refuses to accept the cultural norms denigrating women. As a result, her husband divorces her by simply stating the word *divorce* three times, as is accepted custom. He also takes away her nineteen-month-old son whom she is still nursing.

In *Dancing in the Mosque*, Qaderi writes a letter in exile to a son she is no longer allowed to see. She knows that her son has been told that she, his mother, is dead, and she is forbidden to even see photos of him. She is exiled not only by her husband but by the strict rules of her patriarchal culture. She writes to her son:

My dear Siawash,

Losing you was the most severe pain I have ever suffered and I know you must be very very angry. But I felt I had to make a choice, not just for myself, but also for my country and, ultimately, for you. I don't want either of us to belong to a society that degrades women the way the Afghan society does. You, my son, are a new generation and it is my deepest hope that by the time you grow up, things will have changed—that you will become an instrument of that change.

I always have and always will want to be a mother for you, but I also need to remain Homeira for myself. I could not trade my name for a number; I could not sacrifice my freedom or my dignity. I could not become just another humiliated woman, banished to the supposed sanctuary of our home. I cannot die under a blanket as an angry pitiful, desolate woman. I am trying to save myself and, by doing that, perhaps save other women as well.[24]

Qaderi makes the ultimate sacrifice as a mother. She is forced to give up her son when she rejects a secondary role in her Afghan family. She is exiled by her family and culture when she refuses to submit to its ingrained misogyny. Her hope is that by writing her memoir and telling her story, other Afghani women will stand up for their rights as well.

Whether a person chooses exile like Qian Julie Wang or Azar Nafisi; is exiled due to a culture's customs, like Qaderi; or experiences generational trauma, like Najla Said and George Uba, ultimately we are *all* exiles to a certain extent, looking for a place and community in which to belong. Some people feel like they have been exiled from friends when they go through a divorce, exiled from family members who reject their sexual orientation, or exiled from their profession if they lose their job. Others feel exiled by friends and family for holding certain political beliefs. Eavan Boland writes, "Exile, like memory, may be a place of hope and delusion. But there are rules of light there and principles of darkness, something like a tunnel, in fact. The further you go in, the less you see, the more you know your location by a brute absence of destination."[25]

CRAFTING YOUR MEMOIR

REFLECTION AND TAKEAWAY

One of the key elements of memoir writing is self-reflection. The essence of memoir is tracking a person's thoughts struggling to achieve some understanding of a particular life event. If you take the time to write about a particular memory, the reader wants to know what it means to you. Has it helped you examine the choices you have made in your life? Have you written it in such a way that your reader can identify with you? Without self-reflection, you do not connect on a deeper level with your reader. You might write a beautiful scene, but the reader wants to know how you felt and what you thought. What is your emotional truth? The memoirist and publisher of She Writes Press, Brooke Warner, teaches that "reflection is a moment of inner musing— thoughts and feelings written for the express purpose of making sense of the experience."[26]

An example of reflection is from *Safekeeping* by Abigail Thomas. In a vignette called "A Simple Solution," she describes a scene in New York in the 1970s in which she used to put her dirty feet in the tub when she was bathing her three young children. Her middle daughter complained each night because Thomas went barefoot in Manhattan and picked up all sort of city dirt. More than her dirty feet, however, her daughter felt that Thomas refused to listen to her feelings. Thomas writes, "She says I did this over her protests night after night. I did not, I want to say, but I think she's right. It rings a bell. I didn't understand what was so bad. Perhaps I wanted to be one of the kids instead of the mother. Forgive me. There are so many things I would never do again."[27]

Thomas reflects on the fact that she ignored her daughter's pleas; she didn't want to hear them. She wanted to be a child too.

"Takeaway" offers the reader a moment of direct connection with the writer. It sounds like reflection, but takeaway is for the *reader*, whereas reflection is for the *writer*. Ask yourself: What does the writer feel? In *Safekeeping*, Thomas feels a sense of regret. And now, looking back, she says, she wishes she had done things differently. That is what the reader takes away.

In *Drinking: A Love Story*, Caroline Knapp tells the reader that her book is a cautionary tale about alcoholism and how easy it is to become an alcoholic. She uses definitive statements and statements of conviction to describe being an alcoholic: "Almost by definition alcoholics are lousy at relationship. We melt into them in that muddied, liquid way, rather than marching into them with any real sense of strength or self-awareness."[28] It's a cautionary tale, so she makes a point of connecting with the reader to explain everything about the downfalls of an addiction to alcohol.

In *The Year of Magical Thinking*, Joan Didion combines both self-reflection and takeaway. She tells the reader that as a writer, she has always tried to make sense of things, and she is desperate to make sense of her husband's fatal heart attack. However, in this case, words fail her. "This is a case in which I need more than words to find the meaning. This is a case in which I need whatever it is I think or believe to be penetrable, if only for myself."[29] She reflects on the fact that she has always been able to make meaning out of events, but in the case of her husband's death, in her mind, there is no reasonable justification.

The following is an exercise I use at the end of each writing period. I find that it helps me reflect upon what

I have learned from my writing that day and where I want to go next. Answer the following questions in writing in your journal:

What do you know now that you did not know before?

How do you feel (as a result of this writing)?

What more do you want to find out?

WRITING PROMPTS

YOUR EXILE AND / OR BELONGING

Use one or more of these prompts to inspire your writing:

1. Where do you feel you belong?
2. What gives you a sense of belonging? For Alexandra Fuller, it was the forests in Zambia. For Vivian Gornick, it is the West Side of New York where life feels thematic. What is it for you?
3. With whom do you experience a sense of belonging? Family? Friends? Strangers?
4. How have you known when you don't belong anymore?
5. Qian Julie Wang writes, "I wondered if we had left behind the only place in the world that had our people." Where are your people?
6. How have you been exiled—by your family, by your faith, politically?
7. Have you ever felt like you belong in more than one place at once? Describe the sensation.

9

LOSS

The fundamental paradox of loss is it never
disappears.

—KATHRYN SCHULZ, *Lost and Found*

IN *LOST AND FOUND,* the Pulitzer Prize–winner and staff
writer at the *New Yorker* Kathryn Schulz examines the nature
of loss. She reminds us that throughout our lives we experience many losses that precede the final one: loss of innocence,
loss of virginity, loss of a best friend, loss of memory, loss of
physical strength, loss of balance, loss of flexibility, loss of
intellectual aptitude, loss of a longtime home, loss of identity
derived from work, loss of rights, and perhaps above all, the
loss of time—the feeling that there are things left in this world
we may still want to do but we know we don't have the time
to do them.[1]

The nature of loss is that it encompasses the trivial and
the consequential, the merely misplaced and the permanently
gone.[2] She writes, "We lose things because we are flawed,
because we are human, because we have things to lose."[3]

We all experience a variety of losses throughout life. I lose my glasses at least twice a day, which is annoying but not earth-shattering as it was when I lost my ginger cat, Latte, in the debris flow after the Southern California wildfires of 2018. That was tragic; it reminded me that we are ultimately powerless to protect the things we love. Another time, I lost my balance, fell, and shattered my kneecap, which made me feel vulnerable, but nothing compared to the loss I felt when I sold my home of forty-two years where I had raised my children. That was a loss of my youth and my community of friends and neighbors.

Once I lost my six-year-old daughter on the hiking trail up Devil's Postpile in Mammouth Lakes when she decided to go off and explore on her own. Luckily I was able to find her fairly quickly, but that caused me to lose a sense of confidence in myself as a mother. I lost my first love when we divorced in our late twenties, and immediately I felt like a failure. I lost my dignity and sense of competence when I was recently scammed by an experienced scammer, though on the positive side, I did not lose any money. For years I have mourned the loss of my father, who died eleven years ago, because his death left a huge hole in my life. I had relied on his creative energy to motivate me to move forward. What was I to do, a father's daughter, with no father to impress?

Schulz, in writing about how the death of her father affected her, writes that it felt "like a force that constantly increased its reach, gradually encroaching on more and more terrain."[4] She writes,

> *I lost my father last week.* Perhaps because I was still in those early, distorted days of mourning, when so much of the familiar world feels alien and inaccessible, I was struck, as I had never been before, by the strangeness of the phrase.

Obviously, my father hadn't wandered away from me like a toddler at a picnic or vanished like an important document in a messy office. And yet, unlike other oblique ways of talking about death, this one did not seem cagey or empty. It seemed plain, plaintive, and lonely, like grief itself. . . . Over and over, loss calls on us to reckon with universal impermanence—with the baffling, maddening, heartbreaking fact that something that was just here can be, all of a sudden, just gone.[5]

DON'T LOOK BACK

Joan Didion wrote *The Year of Magical Thinking* after her husband, John Dunne, suddenly had a heart attack and dropped dead as she was serving him dinner. They had just returned from visiting their daughter Quintana, who was in a coma in the ICU at Beth Israel Hospital North in Manhattan. Didion writes about her attempt to make sense of the period that followed his death, about her delusions about her ability to bring him back, about her grief and the ways in which people do and do not deal with death.

The *New York Times* had been alerted, but she didn't want anyone at the *Los Angeles Times* to know that her husband had died because maybe there could be a different ending to the story on Pacific time. Thinking like a small child, she thought her wishes had the power to change the ending.

The man at the hospital where John was pronounced dead asked her if she was willing to donate his organs. She immediately said no. "How could he come back if they took his organs, how could he come back if he had no shoes?"[6] Several months later, a friend offered to help her clean out John's closets. But after gathering his clothes to donate to St. James

Episcopal Church across the street, she could not give away his shoes.

I stopped at the door to the room.
I could not give away the rest of his shoes.
I stood there for a moment, then realized why: he would need shoes if he was to return.
The recognition of this thought by no means eradicated the thought.[7]

Didion makes a distinction between the grief one feels when the death of the loved one is inevitable, like the death of an aged parent, and the grief one feels with the sudden loss of a seemingly healthy loved one. It is not what we expect it to be.

Grief comes in waves, paroxysms, sudden apprehensions that weaken the knees and blind the eyes and obliterate the dailiness of life. Virtually everyone who has ever experienced grief mentions this phenomenon of "waves."[8]

Didion shares a journey with the mythical Orpheus, who eventually lost his head in grief.

Orpheus was the renowned bard of Greek mythology, and his passionate plea to the gods of the underworld to return his wife, Eurydice, to him is so powerful that the myth lives on today in opera, dance, and even the Broadway musical *Hadestown*.

The day of their marriage, Eurydice was bitten by a snake and immediately dropped dead. Orpheus was so gripped by despair and grief that he sang his way into the underworld, playing his lyre for Charon and Cerberus, who let him pass.

When he reached the underworld, he begged Hades and Perse-phone to allow him to take Eurydice back with him to earth. His song charmed them to such a degree that they were moved to tears. Hades agreed to allow Orpheus to take Eurydice with him on one condition: that she walk behind him and that he never look back to see if she was there until they both were out of the underworld.

According to Virgil and Ovid, just as Orpheus entered the last passage of his journey and could see light up ahead, he couldn't contain himself anymore. He turned around to see if Eurydice was following him, and in that moment, she slipped away, falling back into the underworld. Orpheus tried to retrieve her, but he was not allowed to cross the river Styx again. All of his music could not prevail. He sat on the bank of the river for seven days, until he became all but a voice-less skeleton. Eventually the Maenads tore him to pieces and threw his head into the river Hebrus, where it went on singing.

Like Orpheus, Joan Didion did all the rituals to bring her husband back. Nine months after his death, she reflected on how she had done all the right practices to retrieve him: the Catholic priest, the Episcopal priest, the "*In paradisum dedu-cant angeli.*" But no matter what she did, nothing brought him back. Didion herself became skeletal.

People who have lost someone look naked because they think themselves invisible. I, myself, felt invisible for a period of time, incorporeal. I seemed to have crossed one of those legendary rivers that divide the living from the dead, entered a place in which I could be seen only by those who were themselves recently bereaved. I under-stood for the first time the power in the image of the rivers, the Styx, the Lethe, the cloaked ferryman with his pole.[9]

It is one thing to lose one's spouse or parent to death but a much greater loss still to experience the death of a child. Our children are not supposed to predecease us. Mark, the young son of the author Elaine Pagels and her husband, Heinz, died at age six from pulmonary hypertension, a terminal lung disease. In *Why Religion?* Pagels writes that she had always taken it for granted that death was the end and that any thought of surviving death was only a fantasy. But Mark's death challenged her assumptions. The day he died, she felt both his relief at leaving his exhausted body as well as his presence lingering outside of his body.

Pagels and her husband stayed in the hospital room for six or seven hours while death changed Mark's body and features. When they saw that his body had been fully deserted, Heinz said, "It's time to go home." There was nothing more they could do. Knowing that Mark no longer had to struggle didn't change Pagels's feelings of utter loss and devastation, but it gave her a new understanding of their ongoing connection beyond death.

She was both amazed and grateful when so many friends they had not seen for years came to the service for Mark, yet she also felt naked and utterly defenseless.

We stood at the back of the church, weeping and hugging our friends. Standing there, I seemed to see the whole scene embraced by a huge net made of ropes, with enormous spaces between the knots, through which we could be swept away at any moment, out of the world. . . . Yet in that vision, or whatever it was, I felt that the intertwined knots were the connections with the people we loved, and that nothing else could have kept us in this world.[10]

Knowingly or unknowingly, Pagels's experience in the back of the church describes Indra's net, which in Buddhist and Hindu cosmology symbolizes the universe as a web of connections and interdependence. When Indra fashioned the world, he made it as a web, and at every knot in the web he tied a jewel. In this metaphor, Indra's net has a multifaceted jewel at each vertex, and each jewel, glittering like a star, is reflected in all the other jewels in the net. Each one simultaneously reflects every other jewel, ad infinitum. Within each jewel, therefore, is reflected the whole net. Everything and everyone that exists or has ever existed is a jewel in Indra's net.

Feeling her connection to all her loved ones and to all those who had lost children, Pagels's heart began to heal. "My own experience of the nightmare—the agony of feeling isolated, vulnerable, and terrified—has shown that only awareness of that sense of interconnection restores equanimity, even joy."[11]

Both Didion and Pagels write about the feeling of being naked, defenseless, skeletal, unsafe without their loved one at their side to buffer the challenges of living. They long for that sense of companionship during the darkest days of despair. Elaine and Heinz kept each other afloat as their child moved closer to death. But a second loss, totally unexpected, ignited shock beyond anything Pagels had ever imagined.

THE UNIMAGINABLE

One year after Mark's death, Heinz, an accomplished hiker, had an accident descending from Pyramid Peak in Colorado where the family had gone for the summer. The rocky path under his feet gave way, and Heinz fell one thousand feet to his death, his body shattering on the rocks. Like Joan Didion, Pagels could not accept that her husband was gone. When told the news, she could not speak. She went to bed and lay awake, alert, expecting him to return. She believed that as long as she did not sleep, he could return.

A week later, she found boils erupting all over her body. When a doctor asked her what had happened, she said, "I got through our son's death; I'll get through this." The doctor looked at her and said, "This is what we call acute traumatic stress reaction. Don't think that having survived your son's death makes you an expert. Actually, that makes it much worse."[12] Pagels's boils all over her body were a metaphor for the explosions of her anger that had no outlet.

One of the side effects of losing a loved one is murderous rage. "What did I do to deserve this?" "How could they leave me?" "What am I going to do now?" Yes, there's sadness, but underneath that sadness is anger. As a young mother, I was confused when my Irish American grandmother ranted on and on about her husband's death. I never saw her cry about the death of my grandfather. I only felt her fury as she demanded, "Where did you go, Joe?" "How dare you leave me?" "What right did you have to leave?" She survived him by thirty years yet continued, until her death, to blame him for leaving her. Only then did I realize his death replicated the loss she felt when abandoned on a stoop as a five-year-old child by her immigrant parents.

The Greek grain goddess Demeter was so angry when her daughter Persephone was abducted into the underworld that she laid famine all over the earth. For nine days and nine nights she searched everywhere for Persephone. When she learned she was in the underworld and that her consort, Zeus, had ordained the abduction, she was furious. She declared that the whole earth could burn to the ground until she got her daughter back. She then went into deep state of grief and while she mourned, nothing grew on the land. Because the other gods and goddesses received no offerings of wheat or wine while Demeter grieved, they begged Zeus to restore Persephone to her mother. It was only Demeter's rage and grief that brought her daughter back from the dead. One can understand how Pagels's manifestation of boils was akin to Demeter's threat to incinerate the earth.

GUILT

Pagels asks why we feel guilty when a loved one dies. Even when we've done everything humanly possible to prevent their death, we punish ourselves with the illusion that somehow we could have done more. During the last days of her child's illness, Pagels couldn't help imagining that somehow she had caused his death. She felt like a failure as a mother to let her child die and a failure as a wife not to protect her husband. Upon reflection, she realized that she had absorbed cultural messages from Jewish and Christian traditions that preached guilt, punishing the aggrieved for their loss. Pagels understood that to release the weight of the guilt she felt, she had to let go of the illusion that she was in control. She had to accept that pain and death are as natural as birth and part of being human. Unlike the goddess Demeter, she did not have the power to bring her loved ones back.

LOSS OF A FRIEND

Gail Caldwell and Caroline Knapp shared a love of rowing, writing, literature, and walking in the woods of New England with their dogs. It was probably the deepest friendship either woman had ever had; they shared an attachment more profound than either of them could have imagined. The loss of Knapp to terminal lung cancer cracked Caldwell wide open. In *Let's Take the Long Way Home*, Caldwell writes about her grief in the aftermath of Caroline's death:

> The ravages of early grief are such a shock: wild, erratic, disconsolate. If only I could get to sorrow, I thought, I could do sorrow. I wasn't ready for the sheer physicality of it, the lead-lined overcoat of dull pain it would take months to shake.[13]

Several years following Caroline's death, Caldwell's dog, Clementine, died and her heart was broken all over again. "I know now that we never get over great losses; we absorb them, and they carve us into different, often kinder, creatures."[14]

MEMOIR AS A PORTAL TO HEALING

Losing a loved one to death is the most painful experience possible, and writing about it takes courage. We don't want to look at the loss, and we certainly don't want to relive it. Writing doesn't take away our pain, but it does help us have a different relationship to it. Caldwell writes,

> I know I wrote, though not much of it mattered. . . . Mostly I couldn't bear the indisputable lack of her, or the paltry notion that memory was all that eternal life really meant, and I spent too much time wondering where people got the fortitude or delusion to keep on moving past the static dead.[15]

In *Writing as a Way of Healing*, Louise DeSalvo writes, "In my lifelong project of using my writing to unravel the meaning and the feelings about my past, I have revisited my past one moment at a time. Doing so has recast the meaning and significance of my life, has helped me heal."[16] This is the brilliance of memoir writing. Memory is stored in the details of an event, and feelings are stored in those memories. When we reflect upon an event and allow ourselves to feel the feelings that emerge from that memory, we begin to understand what happened, what we felt about it at the time, and what we feel about it now. Writing about it allows us to experience, maybe for the first time, the feelings we couldn't define and assimilate at the time of the event, diffusing its power over us.

The psychology professor James W. Pennebaker studied the healing property of writing in the brain. He examined brain wave activity in people exploring feelings while they were writing about traumatic events. As they wrote, he found a congruence in brain wave activity between left and right hemispheres. This indicated that both emotional and linguistic information was being processed and integrated simultaneously. He also found that his subjects' heart rates lowered and their immune function improved.[17]

When we write our memories and describe our feelings, we integrate them into our sense of self. When we share our inner understanding of our self, we offer a path for others to understand their own lives as well. Writing from an intensely personal experience, such as living through the death of a child, can be helpful to others. Loss is a universal human experience. It does not separate us from others; it establishes our connection with others and the world. Pagels felt that writing about Mark's death helped her move from despair to recognizing that "every one of us is woven into the mysterious fabric of the universe, and into connection with each other, with all being, and with God."[18]

In writing from our pain, we heal gradually, moving from a sense of powerlessness and confusion to a position of wisdom and power. It is the act of describing one's suffering and having it witnessed by the reader that ultimately brings healing—not only for the writer but for the reader as well. Psychic pain, deep personal loss, and unresolved grief are universal, and as the memoirist recounts their own experience, the reader can acknowledge and honor their pain, loss, and grief too.

Isabel Allende wrote *Paula*, a memoir about her daughter's terminal illness and death, while sitting at her comatose daughter's bedside in the hospital. She had previously written fictional accounts of the lives of her ancestors in *The House of the Spirits* but had thought that her own life had little writing value. Though she could not save her daughter, giving form to her pain in writing allowed her to connect to the previous events in her life that had caused her despair. She writes,

My soul is choking in sand. Sadness is a sterile desert. I plunge into these pages in an irrational attempt to overcome my terror. I think that perhaps if I give form to this devastation I shall be able to help you, and myself, and that the meticulous exercise of writing can be our salvation."[19]

She continued, "I went on writing because I could not stop. I could not let anger destroy me."[20] Through her writing, Allende made meaning out of her life as an exile. Before writing her memoir, she felt her life had no order to it, no purpose or path, only a blind journey. After writing, she realized that the underlying pattern of her life had been one of perpetual loss—loss of her father, loss of family, loss of home, loss of country. She had been exiled to Venezuela after the murder of her uncle, the former Chilean president Salvador Allende. As she sat by her daughter's side, writing, she thanked Paula for giving her the "silence" to examine her path through the world. The process of writing transformed her grief into art.

In writing about an illness or a critical life event, a memoirist has the opportunity to link their feelings, both negative and positive, with the memory. It is not easy to describe the details of pain or trauma when one is going through such an experience; the process of healing has not yet begun. The writer needs time and distance to reflect upon their feelings.

Like Allende, I had the opportunity to sit by my mother's bedside as she died. We had always had a difficult relationship, and each time I wrote about her final hour, I had the opportunity to reflect upon our relationship and examine my experience of her. Until then, I had never admitted to myself the part I had played in the difficulties in our relationship. My mother was a convenient hook upon which I had hung all my fear, anger, and desire; she was a complicated, inconsolable woman. I had tried to understand her and protect myself from her abuse for years and had waited, like so many children do, for some acknowledgment of her culpability. Instead, I found myself asking *her* for forgiveness at her deathbed. I didn't know how healing this spontaneous outburst had been for me until I put it into writing.

When a writer has the courage to host a painful memory, she has a chance to make sense of the suffering and confusion it entails. Suffering clarifies identity and connects us with our deepest selves. The expression of suffering, in any form, is often accompanied by shame. But all feelings need expression, and the insights gained from describing a particular passage in life give us the opportunity to grow as human beings. It is the act of writing, rather than the writing itself, that provides an opportunity to heal. The compassion, regard, and deep respect we grow for ourselves and each other is what creates the shift. Healing can occur for the memoirist as they write about their relationship with another person because, in reality, one is never separate from the other.

As a reader perceives a writer grappling with a particular memory and coming to some slow awareness of its significance, a relationship forms between the reader and the writer and between the reader with their own life as well. Reading another person's memoir gives the reader the opportunity to reflect upon *their* life's memories, possibilities, and chances for renewal. If we can offer each other the comfort and insights of our experience, perhaps what we offer will heal. As Pagels writes, "However it happens, sometimes hearts *do* heal, through what I can only call grace."[21]

The fundamental premise of memoir writing is a belief in the restorative power of telling one's truth. Once told, the writer can begin to move on with their life. Allende may never have been able to release her daughter without guilt had she not written the story of Paula's life and examined her own role as mother in the process. I may never have been able to release my mother without regret had I not written the story of her transition in which she allowed me to participate. I had not looked to memoir for healing, but I found it so.

It is true that we never know exactly what heals a person, but the greatest healing may come in knowing that from our suffering we have comfort to offer each other and that we are not, in fact, alone. This is the gift memoir provides: a vehicle for ordinary people like you and me to explore and come to terms with the mysteries and rituals of life and death.

In *The Light of the World*, the poet Elizabeth Alexander's memoir about the death of her Eritrean husband, Ficre, she writes that she never imagined writing a memoir. She also never imagined it would make its way into the world and connect with so many people. She felt like she was just making sounds—not even words—until they became fragments, then sentences. She reminded herself that "the earth will hold me," even though the earth had been swept out from underneath her.[22] When asked if it was cathartic to write, she said no but that she had written her way through a difficult stretch in the road and that each word was a necessary step forward to the next chapter of her life. She also knew that she would be different when she completed it. She writes,

> Loss is our common denominator. None of us will escape it. None of us will outrun death. What do we do in the space between that is our lives? What is the quality and richness of our lives? How do we move through struggle and let community hold us when we have been laid low. This book had to live someplace outside of the sound of my own voice. . . . It had to be larger than me and my individual love.[23]

Alexander reminds us of how important the memoir community is in holding us through our loss.

CRAFTING YOUR MEMOIR

WRITING ABOUT FAMILY

One day in a memoir class I was teaching while writing this book, my student J said that she has stopped writing her memoir because she fears what her family will say. This is a common fear for memoir writers. "Do you mean that they'll be angry at you for describing your relationship with them?" I asked. "No," she said, "they'll say it didn't happen that way."

"That's true," I said. "It didn't happen that way for them, but it did happen that way for you. That's what's important. They had a different experience of a particular event you may be writing about but that does not negate your memory or your experience. It's your memory, not theirs. And what is important is what meaning you made from that event. In other words, what you know now that you didn't know before."

Each family member has their own angle of perception about truth. Their angle of perception might inform your angle of perception, but if it's not true to your experience, you don't need to claim it as your own. Aaron Raz Link wrote "Things We Don't Talk About" to explore his fears about writing about his family. Thinking about who holds the truth, he writes, "To connect personal experience and the written word is also to teach ourselves and one another that neither truth nor text can be absolute."[24]

At first he was afraid that writing about family was an exercise in irrelevance because he thought the relationships in his family only mattered to him. In other words, "Who cares?" But he came to realize that his personal experience with his mother or his brother was also universal to sons and mothers and between siblings. It reflected what was going on in the culture at the particular time about which he wrote. The discipline of writing about family "is to make connections between *history* and *culture* and lived experience, and between lived experience and text."[25] It taught him how his stories connected with other people's.

Link also feared representing his mother and brother in ways convenient to his purpose but perhaps false to their lives. He writes, "No matter how close we are to our families, we can't really know one another's life."[26] We can only know and tell our own.

Yet if we write for publication, we have to choose how to represent the lives of loved ones in print. I have always been impressed with the way Mary Karr approaches writing about living family members. She suggests not using jargon or labels to describe people. She never labeled her parents alcoholics; she showed herself pouring their vodka down the sink.[27] She also shows her writing to those she writes about before it's published. If you decide to show your writing to a friend or family member and they say it never happened that way, you can then let your reader know how subjective your point of view is. However, other writers, such as the essayist, fiction writer, poet, and teacher Phillip Lopate do not show their writing to anyone they've written about. Lopate cautions that once you invite someone to make changes to your manuscript, they will, and he's not interested in giving them that power.

Remember, the most important thing is to get your writing down on the page. No one else has the power to tell your story.

WRITING PROMPTS

Note: When writing about pain or trauma, be sure to write for no more than fifteen minutes at a time; stretch, walk around, and take frequent breaks. I like to wash dishes when writing painful memories. It soothes me to put my hands in warm water.

Use one of more of these prompts to inspire your writing:

1. Make a list of the losses you have experienced in life, both the mundane and the consequential.
2. Choose a significant loss in your life to write about. Follow the first image that appears to you.
3. What pattern in your life began as a result of this loss?
4. What have been the negative and positive aspects of your loss? What have they taught you?
5. How does writing about loss change your understanding of the event? Of yourself?
6. What is the memory you have been afraid to write about because it involves pain? Take your time and give yourself the opportunity to write just one paragraph.
7. How do you experience loss in your body? Give your body a voice.

10

●

SPIRITUALITY

How do we remain faithful to our own spiritual
imagination and not betray what we know in our
bodies?
—TERRY TEMPEST WILLIAMS, *Leap*

IN *SPIRITUALITY AND THE WRITER*, the memoirist and
critic Thomas Larson stresses the idea that a spiritual experience is an *"experience*, usually marked by a sense of sudden
entry into another dimension" distinct from theological beliefs
and doctrines.[1] In other words, one need not be religious to
have spirituality present in their stories. He goes on to explain
that spiritual memoirs feature a prime *relationship* between
the author and a place, a family, a lover, or the inner self
who longs to be found or is content with being lost.[2] To that
I would add a relationship between a woman and her body,
because for many women, the act of giving birth is a deeply
spiritual experience. Ego dissolves and the woman giving birth
becomes one with creation.

Larson makes the distinction that a classic religious auto-
biographer like Augustine of Hippo looks for the "incomparable nature of God, while the spiritual memoirist looks for the

incomparable nature of the self."[3] Perhaps writing memoir is one way, like fasting or pilgrimage, "to summon the ineffable to say what's unsayable."[4] He believes that there is some event, image, or disjunction that sparks the *longing* for the spiritual for the individual memoirist.[5] He emphasizes "disjunction" and the longing that occurs because of it. "That longing crosses desire with transcendence, what we know is there, what we can't have, *yet we want nonetheless.*"[6]

I appreciate that Larson makes the distinction between those who search for the nature of God and those who long for a relationship with their inner self, because in this chapter I am drawn to those memoirists who find their spiritual connection in *relationship* to the land, nature, the body, loved ones, community, art.

In *Gift from the Sea*, Anne Morrow Lindbergh is guided by an inner spiritual need to find peace within herself in the midst of the tremendous chaos around the kidnapping and murder of her twenty-month-old baby. She finds the spiritual in neither God nor religion but in the timelessness of the ocean, the sand, the shells, the rocks, and the wind. Her intent is to find peace.

> I want a singleness of eye, a purity of intention, a central
> core to my life that will enable me to carry out these obli-
> gations and activities as well as I can. I want, in fact—to
> borrow from the language of the saints—to live "in grace"
> as much of the time as possible. I am not using this term in
> a strictly theological sense. By grace I mean an inner har-
> mony, essentially spiritual, which can be translated into
> outward harmony."[7]

Like Lindbergh, Elaine Pagels finds that a major disruption in her life leads to a spiritual experience. Pagels studied

the Gospel of Thomas in search of comfort after the tragic deaths of her son and husband. She writes that even though we are often unaware of our spiritual potential, the sayings of Thomas urged her to keep seeking the divine light within herself. She quotes one of his sayings: "Within a person of light, there is light. If illuminated, it lights up the whole world; if not, everything is dark."[8] His words seemed to articulate the vision she had seen at her son's memorial. There she had experienced a vision: a web of connection with all the people she and her husband had loved. As mentioned in the previous chapter, her vision describes Indra's net, symbolizing the universe as a web of connections and interdependence. Everything and everyone that exists or has ever existed is a jewel in Indra's net. Pagels writes,

> Emerging from a time of unbearable grief, I felt that such [Thomas's] sayings offered a glimpse of what I'd sensed in that vision of the net. They helped dispel isolation and turn me from despair, suggesting that every one of us is woven into the mysterious fabric of the universe, and into connection with each other, with all being, and with God.[9]

How does a person connect to their own sense of the spiritual? Pagels wrestled with despair over the unfairness of the deaths of both her son and husband and searched for meaning. It was the ancient words from the Gospel of Thomas that inspired her to look within, and it was the image of the web of community that gave her support. Both Lindbergh and Pagels suffered incredible losses, and both turned to an encounter with the sacred for support. Others turn to poetry, music, the arts, nature, pilgrimage, or activism as they seek another dimension for succor.

THE GARDEN OF DELIGHTS

Terry Tempest Williams found her connection to the spiritual growing out of her dialogue with a fifteenth-century Flemish masterpiece in the Prado Museum in Spain. Williams spent seven years studying the landscape of *The Garden of Earthly Delights* by Hieronymus Bosch, trying to understand his depiction of the myths about God, evil, suffering, death, life, and the afterlife. As a child sleeping in her Mormon grandmother's house in Utah, the central panel—the earthly delights, between the panels of heaven and hell—had been hidden from the children because of its depiction of sexuality.

When she visited the Prado and saw *The Garden of Earthly Delights* for the first time, she was stunned and then delighted to see naked bodies cavorting with Eros. They were filled with play, discovery, and youthful curiosity, the sensuality of Eros denied her by her grandmother. Why?

In the process of gazing at this powerful masterpiece, Williams found herself wrestling with her deeply held beliefs as a Mormon, as a wife, and as a woman. In *Leap*, she writes, "Let these pages be my interrogation of faith. My roots have been pleached with the wings of a medieval triptych, my soul intertwined with an artist's vision."[10] For seven years she made pilgrimage to Madrid to stand in front of the painting and interrogate the masterpiece.

In trying to wrap my arms around my own religious beliefs, I am aware I pick and choose what feels right to me, adapting as I go, adopting what I like and discarding what I don't within my own ethical framework, which is a simple one, to help more than harm and contribute to the well-being of my community with love, good works, and compassion. . . . We are holy. All life is holy.[11]

She writes about the wound of being separate from the sacred, the pain of isolation, and the longing for the inner self to be found. Larson calls this a *chasm*: "Spirituality is a chasm between a beckoning, absent reality and where we are stuck, yearning for that reality."[12] Williams renews her vows with her husband in the red-rock desert of Utah before a panel of ancient pictographs. And she renews her connection to spirit through the genius of Hieronymus Bosch, who invited her to seek what was denied her. The painting transcended the physical and filled a space in her that was longing to be found. She comes to a "restoration" of spirit through her relationship with both.

> I choose to believe in the power of restoration, the restoration of our faith, even within my own Church of Jesus Christ of Latter-day Saints. Faith is not about finding meaning in the world, there may be no such thing—faith is the belief in our capacity to create meaningful lives. Hieronymus Bosch put his finger on the wound.[13]

Experiencing one's relationship to spirituality can take many forms, including looking at art and having the courage to enter the artist's vision.

PILGRIMAGE

Cheryl Strayed takes a pilgrimage in order to save herself. It is not a typical pilgrimage to Our Lady of Lourdes or the Camino de Santiago to pray for guidance or healing. It is not a pilgrimage from Utah to Madrid to spend time with a painting. It is a 1,100-mile solo trek along the Pacific Crest Trail from Mexico to Canada to grieve her losses: a marriage of infidelity, divorce, drug dependency, the dispersal of her family, and the greatest disruption of all, the death of her mother. She treks by herself to test herself against nature's authority—and perhaps God's or the Great Spirit's authority—and to document it. She begins to understand that hiking the Pacific Crest Trail is her way back to the person she used to be before her life fell apart. Larson writes, "This longing [to be the person I used to be] is one of the mystical traits of spiritual memoir."[14] Strayed longs to uncover her core self without the recent disruptions of her life.

> I was amazed that what I needed to survive could be car-ried on my back. And, most surprising of all, that I could carry it. That I could bear the unbearable. These realiza-tions about my physical, material life couldn't help but spill over into the emotional and spiritual realm. That my complicated life could be made so simple was astounding. It had begun to occur to me that perhaps it was okay that I hadn't spent my days on the trail pondering the sorrows of my life, that perhaps by being forced to focus on my physical suffering some of my emotional suffering would fade away. By the end of that second week, I realized that since I'd begun my hike, I hadn't shed a single tear.[15]

Strayed faced extreme circumstances while on the trail—weather, animals, humans, getting lost—and she had to over-come her little local limitations. When our very survival is at stake, our sensibilities are sharpened. She learned that she was one with the hills and valleys she traversed, that her material domain merged with her spiritual. "Hikers call this becoming one with the mountain," writes Larson.[16] Strayed was restored by nature.

WRESTLING WITH EGO

My favorite spiritual memoir is *In Buddha's Kitchen*, written by Kimberley Snow, who shows how our daily struggle with petty obsessions can ultimately help us discover the grace inherent in life. Snow had once been an executive chef at the Bluegrass Horse Center in Kentucky, where she had a large staff and ran a tight ship feeding hundreds of people at horse sales. Later in life, after experiencing burnout from teaching women's studies at University of California, Santa Barbara, she found herself at a Tibetan Buddhist retreat looking for enlightenment. There, she ended up volunteering to take over the kitchen when the cook's back went out. Instead of focusing on her breath while sitting on a cushion during meditation, she became obsessed with coordinating the food for sixty-five retreatants at an ashram in Northern California.

One day, the Buddhist teacher, Lama Tashi, found her sitting on the floor of the pantry surrounded by her laptop, portable printer, lists and schedules, and banners of material that said "Potatoes" and "Salads." She had forgotten how much she enjoyed the administrative part of being a chef; the more planning she could do, the better. When asked what she was doing, Snow replied she was planning a food fair for the retreat, with different booths. Lama Tashi looked at her and in his funny way of speaking, said, "Meditating not? Why so much attachment having?"

When she explained that she had been a professional chef he said, "In Tibet. One pot. Big spoon." He picked up a plastic pail from the corner of the pantry and pretended to dish out spoonfuls of food to waiting bowls. She had been so invested in her concept of an original food fair that she couldn't think of anything else. "My attachment is truly staggering," she thought to herself. "You good worker," Lama Tashi said. "But you so busy being you!"[17]

The idea of the food fair came during the middle of morning meditation where she hardly noticed the pain in her knees as she thought about the number of food booths she would create. She realized then that most of her suffering came from wanting control. It was not her constitution to spend days breathing in and breathing out. That changed as the months went by.

> When I wasn't obsessed by physical discomfort, something happened to me in that shrine room. My mind expanded beyond self-involvement. I no longer had an individual consciousness but felt deeply embedded in a group experience that transcended the personal altogether. Suddenly I didn't feel lonely anymore, then realized that I hadn't even known I'd felt isolated, alienated before. The sense of separation had become so total it all but disappeared in my consciousness except as a background landscape I moved through. But as the group practiced together, I seemed part of something ancient, timeless, rooted. Something that reached a level for which I'd always felt a nameless homesickness.[18]

Like Williams, Snow describes the wound of being separate from the sacred so many of us are unaware of until we become present to the here and now.

The award-winning British author Karen Armstrong spent seven years in a Roman Catholic convent in England in the 1960s hoping to find God. When she left the convent in 1969 at the height of the counterculture movement, the world as she had known it had dramatically changed. She spent years struggling to find her place in this new world, failing to achieve a doctorate, being unsuccessful at jobs in the media, and struggling with depression, until she was diagnosed with epilepsy and received proper treatment. As a young woman, she had always struggled to do what she was told to do by others, and after she left the convent, she found herself continuing to follow goals that were not right for her. She was unable to find her own path. She had conformed to modes of thought that often seemed alien, yet she couldn't break free. In *The Spiral Staircase*, she writes, "As a result, I found myself [like Parsifal] in a wasteland, an inauthentic existence, in which I struggled mightily but fruitlessly to do what I was told."[19]

In an effort to find God, Armstrong began studying the sacred texts of Judaism, Christianity, and Islam and found that her true calling was to be a writer. She discovered that the religious quest was not about discovering "the truth" or even "the meaning of life" but rather living as intensely as possible in the here and now. Even though she wrote about the greatest spiritual masters' insistence that God was not another being "out there," she still yearned for a personal God. Thinking she had renounced her belief in a supreme being, she found that she was still clinging to her faith in a God she thought she had left behind. She was clinging to *certainty*.

The Greek Fathers of the church had loved the image of Moses going up the mountain and on the summit being wrapped in an impenetrable cloud. He could not see anything, but he was in the place where God was. This cloud of unknowing was precisely that. It offered no knowledge. I had been expecting the thick mist to part, just a little, and had not really known, with every fiber of my being, that I would never know, would never see clearly. I was still hankering for the "one veritable transitory power."[20]

Armstrong's writing about religions became particularly pertinent after September 11, 2001, when the towers of the World Trade Center in Manhattan were attacked. She sought to help people understand Islam, pointing out that the faith of 1.2 billion Muslims should not be judged by the actions of extremists. She tried to build a bridge between worlds that were at odds with each other. She spoke to senators, congresspeople, members of the State Department, and people at the United Nations to convince them that the current task was to mend our broken world, not succumb to retribution. She writes, "What our world needs now is not belief, not certainty, but compassionate action and practically expressed respect for the sacred value of all human beings, even our enemies."[21]

For Armstrong, Williams, and Strayed, finding spiritual wholeness by unconventional means aptly displays the fluidity of God and spirituality. Could God just be humanity's word for something that completes part of the whole? That makes one strong in oneself? In Armstrong's case, traditional religion is the false puzzle piece that she thinks will complete the whole, but what is truly needed is compassionate action.

Kathleen Norris, a poet living in Brooklyn, moved with her husband to a small town in South Dakota in 1974 after her grandmother died. Her mother, brother, and sisters, who all lived in Honolulu, did not want to hold an estate auction, the usual procedure when beneficiaries of an inheritance on the plains live far away. So Norris and her writer husband offered to move there to manage the farm left by her grandparents. In coming to terms with her inheritance and her vocation as a writer, Norris learned that it is not easy to remain on the plains as a poet. Leaving New York where she had attended several poetry readings a week and moving to South Dakota meant entering a literary desert.

Norris was considered an outsider in the community not only because she is a writer but also because she spent her formative years away. Despite having no family in the area, her roots go deep. She says she moved to South Dakota to *hear* her grandmother's voice. "It was a search for inheritance, for place. It was also a religious pilgrimage; on the ground of my grandmother's faith I would find both the means and the end of my search."[22]

She joined her grandmother's Presbyterian church and began visiting monasteries in the desert. It astonished her that the Dakota grasslands led her to a religious frontier where new growth was fed by the fifteen-hundred-year tradition of Benedictine monasticism. It grounded her.

> It was in moving back to the Plains that I found my old ones, my flesh and blood ancestors as well as the desert monks and mystics of the Christian church. Dakota is where it all comes together, and surely that is one definition of the sacred.[23]

Norris discovers that the spareness of the Plains forces her inward. In *Dakota: A Spiritual Geography*, she writes, "The beauty of the Plains is like that of an icon; it does not give an inch to sentiment or romance . . . what seems stern and almost empty is merely open, a door into some simple and holy state."[24] The drastic change in landscape she experiences is, for her, an opening to a spiritual dimension.

She also finds that the hospitality of the monks she visits is an invitation to new self-awareness. "The greatest gift of the monastic tradition, beginning with the desert stories that contain some of the best theology I know, and continuing with my own experience of the Benedictines, is how easily and even beautifully theology converts into experience, and vice versa."[25]

In thinking about Norris, I am reminded of what Larson wrote about a spiritual experience "being marked by a sense of sudden entry into another dimension distinct from theological beliefs and doctrines." For Norris, the plains act as the vehicle for entry into another dimension along with her receptivity to the hospitality and rituals of the Benedictine monks.

The classic sign of [our] acceptance of God's mystery is welcoming and "making room" for the stranger, the other, the surprising, the unlooked-for and unwanted. It means learning to read the world better, that we may better know our place in it.[26]

ONENESS

Dani Shapiro was raised in an Orthodox Jewish household that was steeped in religious ritual. There were rules for everything: eating, speaking, sleeping, praying. She didn't know why her parents did what they did; they never explained it. She had a yeshiva education, prayed in Hebrew, and then, as a teenager, fled everything that was Jewish, replacing it with nothing.

But when she and her husband moved from New York to Connecticut after her young son survived a serious illness, she began a search for a rabbi and a congregation—a place to belong as a Jew. Her desire to belong to a shul was tied up with her gratitude for her son's survival and her love of her very devout father, who died when she was a young woman. "I didn't know how to pray. I knew the Hebrew words and melodies of my childhood—I could recite siddur by heart—but I didn't know what any of it meant. Perhaps Hebrew itself was a samskara. Perhaps one day, while in a deep yoga pose, it would all come flooding back."[27] In *Devotion*, she describes her experience while doing yoga.

> On rare occasions, I felt something else. Something different. It was a sense, not of presence, but of oneness. There was no difference between me and it—nothing separating me from the invisible fabric that made up everything around me. When this happened, it did not feel revelatory. There were no violins, no exploding lights. There was nothing epiphanic, orgiastic, ecstatic, about it. It was a very quiet sense of *knowing*. The words accompanying this knowledge did not strike me as ridiculous. They did not strike me as anything at all, but rather, emerged from a place beyond self-consciousness. *Please allow my heart to open to all that is.*[28]

Like other memoirists who write about a spiritual awakening, Shapiro describes an encounter with another dimension through her senses. She calls it a sense of oneness.

In *Diving Deep and Surfacing*, the feminist thealogian Carol P. Christ describes the spiritual experience for women as an "awakening," often as a result of a mystical experience, a union, or oneness with powers. She writes, "Women often describe their awakening as a coming to self, rather than a giving up of self, as a grounding of selfhood in the powers of being, rather than a surrender of self to the powers of being."[29] Like Terry Tempest Williams who wrote, "The world is holy. We are holy. All life is holy," Christ knew from the time she was a young girl that the earth is holy. In *Laughter of Aphrodite* she writes,

My feelings about the earth spring from mystical experiences, both ordinary and extraordinary, that I have had with nature. There are moments when my connection to a bird, a tree, the sun, a stream, seems undeniable. I have always understood what the Jewish theologian Martin Buber meant when he spoke of having as "I-Thou" relationship with a tree or a piece of mica."[30]

Christ became inspired by ancient Goddess cultures because their symbolism united two themes in her own scholarly work: woman and nature. Her initiation into the symbols and rituals of Goddesses began as a result of being silenced within patriarchal religious and academic structures and a desire for a female God language. She writes, "In retrospect, I would name the night when I heard a still small voice saying, 'God is a woman like yourself,' as the beginning of my initiation into the mysteries of the Goddesses."[31]

Christ decided to move to Lesbos, the birthplace of Sappho, so that she could live in a culture that honored the Goddess. She was drawn to the Minoan Snake Goddess, who was discovered in 1903 at Knossos on Crete. The Snake Goddess, with snakes wrapped around her arms, invokes the power of snakes, a force of regeneration. The Goddess culture in Crete (3000–1500 B.C.E.) was a free, joyous society where men and women coexisted in peace and harmony with nature. The Cretans saw the supreme divine power in terms of the feminine principle. There were symbols of the fertility, sexuality, and abundance of the Goddess painted on the walls of the palace-shrines. The artistic tradition of Crete was unique in the Mediterranean world; artists captured the essential spirit of creatures, such as dolphins leaping in the azure sea. Play and a deep connection to creative eros was the underlying principle of Minoan culture. The Cretans worshipped the Goddess, the mistress of animals and the sea, in mountain-peak shrines and caves that were places of healing. Caves, like the womb of the Goddess, were associated with childbirth and the maternal nature of the divine feminine. Even in the twenty-first century, women still visit the sacred caves to pray for fertility and protection in childbirth.

Christ embodied the spirit of the Goddess by creating and leading groups of women in rituals at caves, at the sites of the temple of Demeter and Persephone at Eleusis, the temple of Artemis at Ephesus, and the temple of Aphrodite in Mesa, Lesbos. She writes, "The presence of the Goddess in these rituals at ancient sites of worship, and in other celebrated closer to home, has created connections spiraling back through time."[32] The discovery of the Paleolithic Minoan Snake Goddess in the twentieth century illustrates the enduring presence of the sacred feminine throughout millennia.

Carol P. Christ has an awakening inspired by the Goddess and makes a geographical move so that she can participate in a culture that honors the sacred feminine. Anne Morrow Lindbergh longs for an inner harmony, essentially spiritual, which can be translated into outward harmony as she is soothed by nature. Elaine Pagels experiences a web that shows all living beings connected to each other in the mysterious fabric of the universe, which gives her comfort. Kimberley Snow experiences a connection to something ancient, timeless, rooted as she sits on a cushion with others breathing in and breathing out. Terry Tempest Williams writes about restoration of the sacred through the art of a fifteenth-century master, and Cheryl Strayed feels the symbiosis of the material and the spiritual as she hikes the trail. Karen Armstrong asks for compassion for the "other" in the midst of political chaos, and Kathleen Norris finds her connection to the spiritual in the openness of the plains of South Dakota.

The words these memoirists find to describe the spiritual realm—grace, inner harmony, interconnection, restoration, symbiosis of material and spiritual, compassion, openness, knowing, oneness, homesickness, awakening—all convey a longing for connection to the ineffable. The unsayable describing the ineffable.

CRAFTING YOUR MEMOIR

WHAT MATTERS?

The memoirist Sven Birkerts found that when he started to write memoir, the events he thought were important and should have left the greatest impression— loves, friendships, trips, deaths—were not the ones that stuck in his memory. He had to ask himself, "What matters?"

As you come to the end of this book, how do you choose what to write? What memory is calling you? What image keeps nudging you? Remember that you don't have to know how your memoir will evolve. Just explore the image, memory, or emotion that keeps you up at night. And follow it. Let it take you to what comes next. Write one word after the other. Let go of your agenda.

The road to truth is not always paved by facts. Although memoir draws primarily from memory, memory and imagination coexist in the mind, and it is important to give yourself permission to untangle the threads of your life with every tool at your disposal. Vivian Gornick was once criticized for her use of composite characters in her memoir *Fierce Attachments*, which is structured around her walks with her mother in New York City. She admitted that she had "composed" some of the walks and conversations with her mother in order to move the narrative forward. What mattered was what she discovered about her relationship with her mother, not the historical truth of their conversations. The discovery she made was that she could not *leave* her mother because she had *become* her mother, unconsciously reflecting the attachment described in the myth of Demeter and Persephone. As Gornick writes in *The Situation and the Story*, "What happened to the writer is not what matters; what matters is the large sense that the writer is able to make of what happened."[33]

Memoir writing is healing because it provides the potential to experience and transform emotions attached to past wounds that were never integrated before. In the process of writing about the past, you have the opportunity not only to recover your past but to experience a sense of reunion and release. So, my question to you is: What matters to you? At this point in time, what memory do you want to explore? And what will you make of it?

Write the story your soul wants to write.

WRITING PROMPTS

YOUR SPIRITUALITY

Use one or more of these prompts to inspire your writing:

1. How do you experience spirituality for yourself?
2. Have you developed a practice to connect you to the spiritual as you define it? Is it a solo practice or is it important for you to practice in community?
3. Have you ever had what you consider a mystical experience?
4. Was your spiritual experience prompted by a loss in your life? By a longing?
5. Do you have a connection to a personal god or goddess?
6. Is an exploration of the inner self imperative for a relationship with the divine?
7. Many people experience a sense of the numinous when they listen to music. Have you found a particular piece of music or a work of art that you associate with the numinous?

List of Writing Prompts

I recommend considering the prompts at the end of each chapter as you read through the book so that information on relevant myths, themes, and archetypes are fresh in your mind. But if you are ever feeling "stuck" in your writing, you can also refer back to the writing prompts listed here any time—turning to whichever category calls to you—to find inspiration and a starting point for your memoir or personal self-exploration.

GETTING STARTED

1. Is there a particular ancient myth or mythological character with whom you identify?
2. Perhaps you recognize something of yourself in that character's journey?
3. Of Campbell's four domains of myth, described on page 5, which are you most drawn to?
4. Archetypal themes such as separation, loss of innocence, trials, failure, betrayal, love, and despair are often present in myth and memoir. Which archetypes would your story include?
5. A personal myth addresses itself to our past, present, and future as well as our identity and purpose in the world. What is your personal myth?
6. What is the family myth handed down by your parents and grandparents?
7. What part of the family myth do you carry?

YOUR ORIGIN STORY

1. Where were you born? How does your birthplace continue to inform your life today?
2. Flor Fernandez Barrios tells us she was named for St. Thérèse, "the Little Flower." What were you told about your name?
3. How do you identify with your culture, race, gender?
4. What is your obligation to your ancestors?
5. What do you know about yourself to be true?
6. Has there been a secret you have carried for your parents? What is it and how has it affected you?
7. How does your story or memoir reflect current issues in your culture?

YOUR PEOPLE

1. How would you describe your parents or guardians, your grandparents?
2. Wolff uses the metaphor of the massive heads of the Easter Islanders' huge sculptures to describe the psychological size of his father. Is there a metaphor that describes your father?
3. Trethewey uses the metaphor of the yellow narcissi to describe her relationship with her mother. What metaphor or artifact represents your relationship with your mother?
4. What draws you to the stories of your ancestors?
5. What guidance did your mother or father give you? How does it continue to live in you?
6. What is the gift given to you by your forebears? My father gave me the pocket watch given to him by his

father, who died before I was born. It had value to me not only as a keepsake but also as representation of the energy of these two creative men.

7. What happens when you hold on to silence?

YOUR LIFE JOURNEY

1. What obstacles have you faced along your journey? How did you overcome them?
2. Have you ever felt betrayed by a loved one? How did that experience make you feel?
3. What did you learn about yourself from dealing with adversaries in your life?
4. Describe a time when you, like Caroline Knapp, hit rock bottom.
5. What sacrifice did you make along your way?
6. Chanel Miller found that there were invisible allies all over the country supporting her. Who have been the allies in your life?
7. Have you ever been silenced? How did you overcome being silenced?

YOUR PURPOSE

1. Mary Jane Nealon knew she was called to be a nurse at an early age. How and where were you called? How did you feel?
2. What decision did you make as a result of this calling?
3. What pattern in your life began as a result of this call?
4. James McBride wanted to explore his roots as a half-Jewish, half-Black man. What do you want to find out about your roots?

5. Like Carolyn Butcher, is there something you came into this world to mend in your family?
6. What is the Big Truth you feel you can't write about?
7. What narrative question does your memoir seek to answer?

YOUR BODY AND WOUNDS

1. How and where were you wounded? How did it feel?
2. What does your body remember?
3. How has your body been marked?
4. Odysseus is recognized by the scar he carries on his thigh. It marks his identity. Do you have a scar that marks your identity?
5. What story does your body yearn to tell?
6. What is trying to be born in you from that wounding?
7. Chanel Miller writes about the personal and cultural wounds we do not see. Have you participated in ignoring those wounds?

YOUR HOME

1. What does an image of home evoke for you?
2. How do you define home? Is it a place, a person, a landscape, a feeling in your body?
3. Describe a dream about home.
4. What remains when home is lost?
5. Have you ever felt like you didn't have a true home? Describe that sensation. Where did it lead you?
6. Where have you found your greatest sense of home?
7. How do you come home to yourself?

YOUR EXILE AND/OR BELONGING

1. Where do you feel you belong?
2. What gives you a sense of belonging? For Alexandra Fuller, it was the forests in Zambia. For Vivian Gornick, it is the West Side of New York where life feels thematic. What is it for you?
3. With whom do you experience a sense of belonging? Family? Friends? Strangers?
4. How have you known when you don't belong anymore?
5. Qian Julie Wang writes, "I wondered if we had left behind the only place in the world that had our people." Where are your people?
6. How have you been exiled—by your family, by your faith, politically?
7. Have you ever felt like you belong in more than one place at once? Describe the sensation.

YOUR LOSS

Note: When writing about pain or trauma, be sure to write for no more than fifteen minutes at a time; stretch, walk around, and take frequent breaks. I like to wash dishes when writing painful memories. It soothes me to put my hands in warm water.

1. Make a list of the losses you have experienced in life, both the mundane and the consequential.
2. Choose a significant loss in your life to write about. Follow the first image that appears to you.

3. What pattern in your life began as a result of this loss?
4. What have been the negative and positive aspects of your loss? What have they taught you?
5. How does writing about loss change your understanding of the event? Of yourself?
6. What is the memory you have been afraid to write about because it involves pain? Take your time and give yourself the opportunity to write just one paragraph.
7. How do you experience loss in your body? Give your body a voice.

YOUR SPIRITUALITY

1. How do you experience spirituality for yourself?
2. Have you developed a practice to connect you to the spiritual as you define it? Is it a solo practice or is it important for you to practice in community?
3. Have you ever had what you consider a mystical experience?
4. Was your spiritual experience prompted by a loss in your life? By a longing?
5. Do you have a connection to a personal god or goddess?
6. Is an exploration of the inner self imperative for a relationship with the divine?
7. Many people experience a sense of the numinous when they listen to music. Have you found a particular piece of music or a work of art that you associate with the numinous?

Notes

INTRODUCTION

1. Joseph Campbell, with Bill Moyers, *The Power of Myth* (New York: Doubleday, 1988), 5.

CHAPTER 1: ANCIENT MYTH, CONTEMPORARY MEMOIR

1. Terry Tempest Williams, *Leap* (New York: Pantheon Books, 2000), 88.
2. Patricia Hampl, *I Could Tell You Stories: Sojourns in the Land of Memory* (New York: W. W. Norton, 1999), 18.
3. Dani Shapiro, *Inheritance: A Memoir of Genealogy, Paternity, and Love* (New York: Alfred A Knopf, 2019), 63.
4. Joan Didion, *The Year of Magical Thinking* (New York: Alfred A. Knopf, 2005), 33.
5. Robert A. Segal, introduction to *Jung on Mythology* (Princeton, NJ: Princeton University Press, 1990), 16.
6. Brando Skyhorse, *Take This Man: A Memoir* (New York: Simon & Schuster, 2014), 1.
7. Toni Morrison, *What Moves at the Margin: Selected Nonfiction*, ed. Carolyn C. Denard (Jackson, MS: University Press of Mississippi, 2008), 73.

CHAPTER 2: WHO AM I? CREATION MYTHS

1. Robin Wall Kimmerer, *Braiding Sweetgrass: Indigenous Wisdom, Scientific Knowledge, and the Teachings of Plants* (Minneapolis, MN: Milkweed Editions, 2013), 305.

2. Marie-Louise von Franz, *Creation Myths* (Boston: Shambhala Publications, 1995), 29.

3. Anne Cross, *The Raven and the First Men: From Conception to Completion,* University of British Columbia Museum of Anthropology Pacific Northwest Sourcebook Series (Vancouver, BC: UBC Museum of Anthropology, 2011).

4. Flor Fernandez Barrios, *Blessed by Thunder: Memoir of a Cuban Girlhood* (Seattle, WA: Seal Press, 1999), 3.

5. Jana Zimmer, *Chocolates from Tangier: A Holocaust Replacement Child's Memoir of Art and Transformation.* (Los Angeles: DoppelHouse Press, 2023), 69.

6. Jeanette Winterson, *Why Be Happy When You Could Be Normal?* (New York: Grove Press, 2011), 220.

7. Winterson, *Why Be Happy When You Could Be Normal?,* 223.

8. Jeanette Winterson, *Oranges Are Not the Only Fruit* (New York: Grove Press, 1985), 164.

9. Maureen Murdock, *Unreliable Truth: On Memoir and Memory* (New York: Seal Press, 2003), 55.

10. Honor Moore, *The Bishop's Daughter: A Memoir* (New York: W. W. Norton, 2008), 9.

11. Moore, *Bishop's Daughter,* 332.

12. Moore, 332.

13. Dani Shapiro, *Inheritance: A Memoir of Genealogy, Paternity, and Love* (New York: Alfred A. Knopf, 2019), 35.

14. Shapiro, *Inheritance,* 30–31.

15. Alex Marshall, "Annie Ernaux's Work Dissecting the Deeply Personal Is Awarded the Nobel," *New York Times,* October 6, 2022, www.nytimes.com/2022/10/06/books/annie-ernaux -nobel-prize-literature.html.

CHAPTER 3: WHO ARE MY PEOPLE?

1. Dani Shapiro, *Inheritance: A Memoir of Genealogy, Paternity, and Love* (New York: Alfred A. Knopf, 2019), 12.

2. Terry Tempest Williams, *Leap* (New York: Pantheon Books, 2000), 177.

3. Wayétu Moore, *The Dragons, the Giant, the Women: A Memoir* (Minneapolis, MN: Graywolf Press, 2020), 55–56.

4. Christine Downing, *The Long Journey Home: Re-Visioning the Myth of Demeter and Persephone for Our Time* (Boston: Shambhala Publications, 1994), 222.

5. J (unpublished work).

6. Sven Birkerts, *The Art of Time in Memoir: Then, Again* (Minneapolis, MN: Graywolf Press, 2008), 118.

7. Natasha Trethewey, *Memorial Drive: A Daughter's Memoir* (New York: Ecco, 202), 72.

8. Trethewey, *Memorial Drive*, 208.

9. James Olney, *Metaphors of Self: The Meaning of Autobiography* (Princeton, NJ: Princeton University Press, 1972), 34.

10. Sarah M. Broom, *The Yellow House* (New York: Grove Press, 2019), 366–67.

11. Geoffrey Wolff, *The Duke of Deception: Memories of My Father* (New York: Vintage Books, 1979), 11.

12. Wolff, *Duke of Deception*, 11.

13. Wolff, 10.

14. Maxine Hong Kingston, *The Woman Warrior: Memoirs of a Girlhood Among Ghosts* (New York: Vintage Books, 1976), 5.

15. Hong Kingston, *Woman Warrior*, 7.

16. Hong Kingston, 7.

17. Hong Kingston, 19.

18. Hong Kingston, 18.

CHAPTER 4: WHAT IS MY JOURNEY?

1. Natasha Trethewey, *Memorial Drive: A Daughter's Memoir* (New York: Ecco, 2020), 15.

2. Joy Harjo, *Crazy Brave: A Memoir* (New York: W. W. Norton, 2012), 20.

3. Kathryn Harrison, *The Kiss: A Memoir* (New York: Avon Books, 1997), 32.

4. Harrison, *Kiss*, 51.

5. Harrison, 68–69.

6. Harrison, 70.

7. Caroline Knapp, *Drinking: A Love Story* (New York: Bantam Dell, 1996), xvi.

8. Knapp, *Drinking*, xvi.

9. Knapp, 5.

10. Knapp, 217.

11. Knapp, 217.

12. Cheryl Strayed, *Wild: From Lost to Found on the Pacific Crest Trail* (New York: Vintage Books, 2013), 156–57.

13. Gail Caldwell, *Let's Take the Long Way Home: A Memoir of Friendship* (New York: Random House, 2010), 4.

14. Chanel Miller, *Know My Name: A Memoir* (New York: Penguin Books, 2020), 166–67.

15. Miller, *Know My Name*, 211–12.

CHAPTER 5: WHAT IS MY PURPOSE?

1. Joy Harjo, *Crazy Brave: A Memoir* (New York: W. W. Norton, 2012), 20.

2. Harjo, *Crazy Brave*, 154.

3. Harjo, 163.

4. Myra Shapiro, *Four Sublets: Becoming a Poet in New York* (Goshen, CT: Chicory Blue Press, 2007), 8–9.

5. Mary Jane Nealon, *Beautiful Unbroken: One Nurse's Life* (Minneapolis, MN: Graywolf Press, 2011), 5.

6. Nealon, *Beautiful Unbroken*, 13.

7. Nealon, 13.

8. James McBride, *The Color of Water: A Black Man's Tribute to His White Mother* (New York: Riverhead Books, 1996), 269.

9. Maureen Murdock, *Unreliable Truth: On Memoir and Memory* (New York: Seal Press, 2003), 74.

10. Natasha Trethewey, *Memorial Drive: A Daughter's Memoir* (New York: Ecco, 2020), 11.

11. Jeanette Winterson, *Why Be Happy When You Could Be Normal?* (New York: Grove Press, 2011), 226.

12. Sven Birkerts, *The Art of Time in Memoir: Then, Again* (Minneapolis, MN: Graywolf Press, 2008), 3–4.

13. Carolyn Butcher, "Make Room for Butterflies" (unpublished manuscript).

14. Birkerts, *Art of Time in Memoir*, 3–4.

15. David Carr, *The Night of the Gun: A Reporter Investigates the Darkest Story of His Life—His Own* (New York: Simon & Schuster, 2008), 10.

16. Carr, *Night of the Gun*, 11.

17. Carr, 9.

18. Dani Shapiro, *Inheritance: A Memoir of Genealogy, Paternity, and Love* (New York: Alfred A. Knopf, 2019), 71.

19. Gail Caldwell, *Let's Take the Long Way Home: A Memoir of Friendship* (New York: Random House, 2010), 123.

20. Caldwell, *Let's Take the Long Way Home*, 182.

21. bell hooks, *Remembered Rapture: The Writer at Work* (New York: Henry Holt and Company, 1999), 84.

CHAPTER 6: WOUNDING AND THE BODY

1. Dennis Patrick Slattery, *The Wounded Body: Remembering the Markings of Flesh* (Albany: State University of New York Press, 2000), 27.

2. Jean-Dominique Bauby, *The Diving Bell and the Butterfly* (New York: Vintage Books, 1998), 97.

3. Bauby, *Diving Bell and the Butterfly*, 3–4.

4. Bauby, 129.

5. Slattery, *Wounded Body*, 53.
6. Jeanette Winterson, *Why Be Happy When You Could Be Normal?* (New York: Grove Press, 2011), 222.
7. Winterson, *Why Be Happy When You Could Be Normal?*, 5.
8. Chanel Miller, *Know My Name: A Memoir* (New York: Penguin Books, 2020), 6–7.
9. Roger L. Green, *Heroes of Greece and Troy* (New York: Walk, 1961): 222.
10. Miller, *Know My Name*, 315.
11. Jeannette Walls, *The Glass Castle: A Memoir* (New York: Scribner, 2005), 9–11.
12. Terry Tempest Williams, *Refuge: An Unnatural History of Family and Place* (New York: Vintage, 1992), 281.
13. Williams, *Refuge*, 161.
14. Williams, 4.
15. Williams, 178.
16. Williams, 44.
17. Sherman Alexie, *You Don't Have to Say You Love Me* (New York: Little, Brown, 2017), 453.
18. Mary Karr, *The Art of Memoir* (New York: HarperCollins, 2015), 71.
19. Walls, *Glass Castle*, 9.

CHAPTER 7: HOME AND HOMECOMING

1. Ami Ronnberg, ed., *The Book of Symbols* (Cologne, Germany: Taschen, 2010), 556.
2. Ginette Paris, *Pagan Meditations: The Worlds of Aphrodite, Artemis, and Hestia* (Dallas, TX: Spring Publications, 1986), 170.
3. Terry Tempest Williams, *Erosion: Essays of Undoing* (New York: Sarah Crichton Books, 2019), 3.
4. Kathleen Norris, *Dakota: A Spiritual Geography* (New York: Houghton Mifflin, 1993), 24.

5. Deborah Levy, *Real Estate: A Living Autobiography* (New York: Bloomsbury, 2021), 3.

6. Gabriel Byrne, *Walking with Ghosts: A Memoir* (New York: Picador, 2020), 1.

7. Jana Zimmer, *Chocolates from Tangier: A Holocaust Replacement Child's Memoir of Art and Transformation* (Los Angeles: DoppelHouse Press, 2023), 225–26.

8. Joan Didion, *The White Album* (New York: Farrar, Straus and Giroux, 2009), 146.

9. Vivian Gornick, *The Odd Woman and the City: A Memoir* (New York: Farrar, Straus and Giroux, 2015), 94–95.

10. Gornick, *Odd Woman and the City*, 68.

11. Gornick, 68.

12. Sarah M. Broom, *The Yellow House* (New York: Grove Press, 2019), 149.

13. Broom, *Yellow House*, 150.

14. Broom, 232.

15. Broom, 225.

16. Broom, 282.

17. Toni Morrison, *Beloved* (New York: Penguin Books, 1988), 35–36.

18. Kathryn Schulz, *Lost and Found* (New York: Random House, 2022), 142.

19. Byrne, *Walking with Ghosts*, 11.

20. Jose Antonio Vargas, *Dear America: Notes of an Undocumented Citizen* (New York: HarperCollins, 2018), 222.

21. Vargas, *Dear America*, 110.

22. Vargas, 109.

23. Vargas, 221.

24. Susan E. King, *Redressing the Sixties: Catalog and Narrative* (Lexington, KY: Paradise Press, 2022), 31.

25. Levy, *Real Estate*, 6.

26. Levy, 3.

1. Qian Julie Wang, *Beautiful Country: A Memoir* (New York: Doubleday, 2021), 3.
2. Wang, *Beautiful Country*, 39.
3. Wang, 33.
4. Wang, 41.
5. Najla Said, *Looking for Palestine: Growing Up Confused in an Arab-American Family* (New York: Riverhead Books, 2013), 164.
6. Said, *Looking for Palestine*, 165.
7. Said, 166.
8. Louise J. Kaplan, *No Voice Is Ever Wholly Lost* (New York: Simon & Schuster, 1995), 225.
9. George Uba, *Water Thicker Than Blood: A Memoir of a Post-Internment Childhood* (Philadelphia: Temple University Press, 2022), 9.
10. Flor Fernandez Barrios, *The Mask of Oyá: A Healer's Journey into the Empowering Realm of Ancestors and Spirits* (self-pub., 2014), 9–10.
11. Fernandez Barrios, *Mask of Oyá*, 23.
12. Sharon O'Brien, *The Family Silver: A Memoir of Depression and Inheritance* (Chicago: University of Chicago Press, 2004), 80.
13. O'Brien, *Family Silver*, 80.
14. Maureen Dezell, *Irish America: Coming into Clover* (New York: Anchor Books, 2002), 85.
15. Eavan Boland, *Object Lessons: The Life of the Woman and the Poet in Our Time* (New York: W. W. Norton, 1995), 50–51.
16. Boland, *Object Lessons*, 55–56.
17. Boland, 56.
18. Boland, 56.
19. Azar Nafisi, *Reading Lolita in Tehran: A Memoir in Books* (New York: Random House, 2003), 316.
20. Nafisi, *Reading Lolita in Tehran*, 316.

21. Nafisi, 330.
22. Alexandra Fuller, *Leaving Before the Rains Come* (New York: Penguin Press, 2015), 225.
23. Fuller, *Leaving Before the Rains Come*, 258.
24. Homeira Qaderi, *Dancing in the Mosque: An Afghan Mother's Letter to Her Son* (New York: Harper, 2020), 202.
25. Boland, *Object Lessons*, 56.
26. Brooke Warner (class handout).
27. Abigail Thomas, *Safekeeping: Some True Stories from a Life* (New York: Anchor, 2001), 38.
28. Caroline Knapp, *Drinking: A Love Story* (New York: Bantam Dell, 1996), 89.
29. Joan Didion, *The Year of Magical Thinking* (New York: Alfred A. Knopf, 2005), 8.

CHAPTER 9: LOSS

1. Kathryn Schulz, *Lost and Found* (New York: Random House, 2022), 38.
2. Schulz, *Lost and Found*, 6.
3. Schulz, 15.
4. Schulz, 5.
5. Schulz, 4, 20.
6. Joan Didion, *The Year of Magical Thinking* (New York: Alfred A. Knopf, 2005), 41.
7. Didion, *Year of Magical Thinking*, 37.
8. Didion, 27.
9. Didion, 75.
10. Elaine Pagels, *Why Religion? A Personal Story* (New York: HarperCollins, 2018), 89.
11. Pagels, *Why Religion?*, 205.
12. Pagels, 118.
13. Gail Caldwell, *Let's Take the Long Way Home: A Memoir of Friendship* (New York: Random House, 2010), 152.

14. Caldwell, *Let's Take the Long Way Home*, 182.
15. Caldwell, 163.
16. Louise DeSalvo, *Writing as a Way of Healing: How Telling Our Stories Transforms Our Lives* (Boston: Beacon Press, 1999), 27.
17. DeSalvo, *Writing as a Way of Healing*, 28.
18. Pagels, *Why Religion?*, 177.
19. Isabel Allende, *Paula: A Memoir* (New York: Harper Perennial, 1996), 9.
20. Allende, *Paula*, 130.
21. Pagels, *Why Religion?*, 211.
22. Elizabeth Alexander, *The Light of the World: A Memoir* (New York: Grand Central Publishing, 2016), 205.
23. Alexander, *Light of the World*, 206.
24. Aaron Raz Link, "Things We Don't Talk About," in *Family Trouble: Memoirists on the Hazards and Rewards of Revealing Family*, ed. Joy Castro (Lincoln: University of Nebraska Press, 2013), 152.
25. Link, "Things We Don't Talk About," 152.
26. Link, 153.
27. Mary Karr, *The Art of Memoir* (New York: HarperCollins, 2015), 120.

CHAPTER 10: SPIRITUALITY

1. Thomas Larson, *Spirituality and the Writer: A Personal Inquiry* (Athens, OH: Swallow Press, 2019), 32.
2. Larson, *Spirituality and the Writer*, 95.
3. Larson, 93.
4. Larson, 99.
5. Larson, 95.
6. Larson, 37.
7. Anne Morrow Lindbergh, *Gift from the Sea* (New York: Pantheon, 1955), 17.

8. Elaine Pagels, *Why Religion? A Personal Story* (New York: HarperCollins, 2018), 177.

9. Pagels, *Why Religion?*, 177.

10. Terry Tempest Williams, *Leap* (New York: Pantheon Books, 2000), 5.

11. Williams, *Leap*, 147.

12. Larson, *Spirituality and the Writer*, 37.

13. Williams, *Leap*, 26.

14. Larson, *Spirituality and the Writer*, 106.

15. Cheryl Strayed, *Wild: From Lost to Found on the Pacific Crest Trail* (New York: Vintage Books, 2013), 92.

16. Larson, *Spirituality and the Writer*, 109.

17. Kimberley Snow, *In Buddha's Kitchen: Cooking, Being Cooked, and Other Adventures in a Meditation Center* (Boston: Shambhala Publications, 2003), 13.

18. Snow, *In Buddha's Kitchen*, 29.

19. Karen Armstrong, *The Spiral Staircase: My Climb Out of Darkness* (New York: Alfred A. Knopf, 2004), 269.

20. Armstrong, *Spiral Staircase*, 301.

21. Armstrong, 304.

22. Norris, *Dakota*, 93.

23. Norris, 131.

24. Norris, 157.

25. Norris, 117.

26. Norris, 198.

27. Dani Shapiro, *Devotion: A Memoir* (New York: Harper Perennial, 2011), 120.

28. Shapiro, *Devotion*, 121.

29. Carol P. Christ, *Diving Deep and Surfacing: Women Writers on Spiritual Quest* (Boston: Beacon Press, 1980), 19.

30. Carol P. Christ, *Laughter of Aphrodite: Reflections on a Journey to the Goddess* (San Francisco: Harper & Row, 1987), x.

31. Christ, *Laughter of Aphrodite*, 184.

32. Christ, *Laughter of Aphrodite*, xi.
33. Vivian Gornick, *The Situation and the Story: The Art of Personal Narrative* (New York: Farrar, Straus and Giroux, 2001), 91.

Bibliography

Alexander, Elizabeth. *The Light of the World: A Memoir*. New York: Grand Central Publishing, 2016.

Alexie, Sherman. *You Don't Have to Say You Love Me: A Memoir*. New York: Little, Brown, 2017.

Allende, Isabel. *Paula*. New York: Harper Perennial, 1996.

Armstrong, Karen. *The Spiral Staircase: My Climb Out of Darkness*. New York: Alfred A. Knopf, 2004.

Barrios, Flor Fernandez. *Blessed by Thunder: Memoir of a Cuban Girlhood*. Seattle, WA: Seal Press, 1999.

Barrios, Flor Fernandez. *The Mask of Oyá: A Healer's Journey into the Empowering Realm of Ancestors and Spirits*. Vancouver: Liaison Press, 2014.

Bauby, Jean-Dominique. *The Diving Bell and the Butterfly*. New York: Vintage Books, 1998.

Birkerts, Sven. *The Art of Time in Memoir: Then, Again*. Minneapolis, MN: Graywolf Press, 2008.

Boland, Eavan. *Object Lessons: The Life of the Woman and the Poet in Our Time*. New York: W. W. Norton, 1995.

Broom, Sarah M. *The Yellow House*. New York: Grove Press, 2019.

Butcher, Carolyn. "Make Room for Butterflies." Unpublished manuscript, 2022.

Byrne, Gabriel. *Walking with Ghosts: A Memoir*. New York: Picador, 2020.

Caldwell, Gail. *Let's Take the Long Way Home: A Memoir of Friendship*. New York: Random House, 2010.

Campbell, Joseph, with Bill Moyers. *The Power of Myth*. New York: Doubleday, 1988.

Carr, David. *The Night of the Gun: A Reporter Investigates the Darkest Story of His Life—His Own.* New York: Simon & Schuster, 2008.

Christ, Carol P. *Laughter of Aphrodite: Reflections on a Journey to the Goddess.* San Francisco: Harper & Row, 1987.

Christ, Carol P. *Diving Deep and Surfacing: Women Writers on Spiritual Quest.* Boston: Beacon Press, 1980.

DeSalvo, Louise. *Writing as a Way of Healing: How Telling Our Stories Transforms Our Lives.* Boston: Beacon Press, 1999.

Dezell, Maureen. *Irish America: Coming into Clover.* New York: Anchor Books, 2002.

Didion, Joan. *The Year of Magical Thinking.* New York: Alfred A. Knopf, 2005.

Downing, Christine. *The Long Journey Home: Re-Visioning the Myth of Demeter and Persephone for Our Time.* Boston: Shambhala Publications, 1994.

Franz, Marie-Louise von. *Creation Myths.* Boston: Shambhala Publications, 1995.

Fuller, Alexandra. *Don't Let's Go to the Dogs Tonight: An African Childhood.* New York: Random House, 2003.

Fuller, Alexandra. *Leaving Before the Rains Come.* New York: Penguin, 2015.

Gathercole, Simon. *The Gospel of Thomas: Introduction and Commentary.* Leiden: Brill Academic, 2014.

Gornick, Vivian. *The Odd Woman and the City: A Memoir.* New York: Farrar, Straus and Giroux, 2015.

Gornick, Vivian. *The Situation and the Story: The Art of Personal Narrative.* New York: Farrar, Straus and Giroux, 2001.

Hampl, Patricia. *I Could Tell You Stories: Sojourns in the Land of Memory.* New York: W. W. Norton, 1999.

Harjo, Joy. *Crazy Brave: A Memoir.* New York: W. W. Norton, 2012.

Harrison, Kathryn. *The Kiss: A Memoir.* New York: Avon Books, 1997.

hooks, bell. *Remembered Rapture: The Writer at Work.* New York: Henry Holt and Company, 1999.

Kaplan, Louise. *No Voice Is Ever Wholly Lost.* New York: Simon & Schuster, 1995.

Karr, Mary. *The Art of Memoir.* New York: HarperCollins, 2015.

Kimmerer, Robin Wall. *Braiding Sweetgrass: Indigenous Wisdom, Scientific Knowledge and the Teachings of Plants.* Minneapolis, MN: Milkweed Editions, 2013.

King, Susan E. *Redressing the Sixties.* Lexington, KY: Paradise Press, 2022.

Kingston, Maxine Hong. *The Woman Warrior: Memoirs of a Girlhood among Ghosts.* New York: Vintage Books, 1976.

Knapp, Caroline. *Drinking: A Love Story.* New York: Bantam Dell, 1996.

Larson, Thomas. *Spirituality and the Writer: A Personal Inquiry.* Athens, OH: Swallow Press, 2019.

Levy, Deborah. *Real Estate: A Living Autobiography.* New York: Bloomsbury, 2021.

Lindbergh, Anne Morrow. *Gift from the Sea.* New York: Pantheon, 1955.

Link, Aaron Raz. "Things We Don't Talk About." In *Family Trouble: Memoirists on the Hazards and Rewards of Revealing Family,* edited by Joy Castro, 146–158. Lincoln: University of Nebraska Press, 2013.

McBride, James. *The Color of Water: A Black Man's Tribute to His White Mother.* New York: Riverhead Books, 1996.

McCourt, Frank. *Angela's Ashes.* New York: Scribner, 1996.

Miller, Chanel. *Know My Name: A Memoir.* New York: Penguin Books, 2020.

Moore, Honor. *The Bishop's Daughter: A Memoir.* New York: W. W. Norton, 2008.

Moore, Wayétu. *The Dragons, the Giant, the Women: A Memoir.* Minneapolis, MN: Graywolf Press, 2020.

Morrison, Toni. *Beloved.* New York: Penguin Books, 1988.

Morrison, Toni. *What Moves at the Margin: Selected Nonfiction.* Edited by Carolyn C. Denard. Jackson, MS: University Press of Mississippi, 2008.

Murdock, Maureen. *The Heroine's Journey: Woman's Quest for Wholeness.* Boulder, CO: Shambhala Publications, 1990.

Murdock, Maureen. *Unreliable Truth: On Memoir and Memory.* New York: Seal Press, 2003.

Nafisi, Azar. *Reading Lolita in Tehran: A Memoir in Books.* New York: Random House, 2003.

Nealon, Mary Jane. *Beautiful Unbroken: One Nurse's Life.* Minneapolis, MN: Graywolf Press, 2011.

Norris, Kathleen. *Dakota: A Spiritual Geography.* New York: Houghton Mifflin, 1993.

O'Brien, Sharon. *The Family Silver: A Memoir of Depression and Inheritance.* Chicago: University of Chicago Press, 2004.

Olney, James. *Metaphors of Self: The Meaning of Autobiography.* Princeton, NJ: Princeton University Press, 1972.

Pagels, Elaine. *Why Religion? A Personal Story.* New York: HarperCollins, 2018.

Paris, Ginette. *Pagan Meditations: The Worlds of Aphrodite, Artemis, and Hestia.* Dallas, TX: Spring Publications, 1986.

Pennebaker, James W. *Opening Up: The Healing Power of Confiding in Others.* New York: Morrow, 1990.

Qaderi, Homeira. *Dancing in the Mosque: An Afghan Mother's Letter to Her Son.* New York: Harper, 2020.

Ronnberg, Ami, ed. *The Book of Symbols: Reflections on Archetypal Images.* Cologne, Germany: Taschen, 2010.

Said, Najla. *Looking for Palestine; Growing Up Confused in an Arab-American Family.* New York: Riverhead Books, 2013.

Schulz, Kathryn. *Lost and Found.* New York: Random House, 2022.

Segal, Robert A., ed. Introduction to *Jung on Mythology*, 16–17. Princeton, NJ: Princeton University Press, 1990.

Selig, Jennifer Leigh, ed. *Writing Down the Soul: Class of 2022.* Sacramento, CA: Mandorla Books, 2023.

Shapiro, Dani. *Devotion: A Memoir*. New York: Harper Perennial, 2011.

Shapiro, Dani. *Inheritance: A Memoir of Genealogy, Paternity, and Love*. New York: Alfred A. Knopf, 2019.

Shapiro, Myra. *Four Sublets: Becoming a Poet in New York*. Goshen, CT: Chicory Blue Press, 2007.

Skyhorse, Brando. *Take This Man: A Memoir*. New York: Simon & Schuster, 2014.

Slattery, Dennis Patrick. *The Wounded Body: Remembering the Markings of Flesh*. Albany: State University of New York Press, 2000.

Snow, Kimberley. *In Buddha's Kitchen: Cooked, Being Cooked, and Other Adventures in a Meditation Center*. Boston: Shambhala Publications, 2003.

Strayed, Cheryl. *Wild: From Lost to Found on the Pacific Crest Trail*. New York: Vintage Books, 2013.

Thomas, Abigail. *Safekeeping: Some True Stories from a Life*. New York: Anchor, 2001.

Trethewey, Natasha. *Memorial Drive: A Daughter's Memoir*. New York: Ecco, 2020.

Uba, George. *Water Thicker Than Blood: A Memoir of a Post-Internment Childhood*. Philadelphia: Temple University Press, 2022.

Vargas, Jose Antonio. *Dear America: Notes of an Undocumented Citizen*. New York: HarperCollins, 2018.

Walls, Jeannette. *The Glass Castle: A Memoir*. New York: Scribner, 2005.

Wang, Qian Julie. *Beautiful Country: A Memoir*. New York: Doubleday, 2021.

Williams, Terry Tempest. *Erosion: Essays of Undoing*. New York: Sarah Crichton Books, 2019.

Williams, Terry Tempest. *Leap*. New York: Pantheon Books, 2000.

Williams, Terry Tempest. *Refuge: An Unnatural History of Family and Place*. New York: Vintage, 1992.

Winterson, Jeanette. *Oranges Are Not the Only Fruit*. New York: Grove Press, 1985.

Winterson, Jeanette. *Why Be Happy When You Could Be Normal?* New York: Grove Press, 2011.

Wolff, Geoffrey. *The Duke of Deception: Memories of My Father*. New York: Vintage Books, 1979.

Zimmer, Jana. *Chocolates from Tangier: A Holocaust Replacement Child's Memoir of Art and Transformation*. Los Angeles: DoppelHouse Press, 2023.

MYTHS AND MYTHIC FIGURES REFERENCED

Asclepius	Minoan Snake Goddess
Athena	Moses
Castor and Pollux	Odysseus and Telemachus
Chiron	Orpheus and Eurydice
Demeter and Persephone	Oyá
Eve and Lilith	Parsifal
Gaia	Prometheus
Helios	Psyche and Eros
Hestia	Raven, the Haida Trickster
Indra's net	Selene
Iphigenia	Uranus and Cronus

REFERENCES ON MYTHS

Aeschylus. *Prometheus Bound and Other Plays*. Translated by Philip Vellacott. New York: Penguin Books, 1961.

Barrios, Flor Fernandez. *The Mask of Oyá: A Healer's Journey into the Empowering Realm of Ancestors and Spirits*. Vancouver: Liaison Press, 2014.

Bolen, Jean Shinoda. *Goddesses in Everywoman: Powerful Archetypes in Women's Lives*. San Francisco: Harper & Row, 1984.

Bond, D. Stephenson. *Living Myth: Personal Meaning as a Way of Life*. Boston: Shambhala Publications, 1993.

Burrows, David J., Frederick R. Lapides, and John T. Shawcross, eds. *Myths and Motifs in Literature*. New York: Free Press, 1973.

Cross, Anne. *The Raven and the First Men: From Conception to Completion*. University of British Columbia Museum of Anthropology Pacific Northwest Sourcebook Series. Vancouver, BC: UBC Museum of Anthropology, 2011.

Downing, Christine. *The Goddess: Mythological Images of the Feminine*. New York: Crossroad, 1981.

Fagels, Robert, trans. *Homer: The Odyssey*. New York: Penguin Books, 1996.

Foley, Helene P. ed. *The Homeric Hymn to Demeter: Translation, Commentary, and Interpretative Essays*. Princeton, NJ: Princeton University Press, 1994.

Franz, Marie-Louise von. *Creation Myths*. Boston: Shambhala Publications, 1995.

Gadon, Elinor W. *The Once and Future Goddess: A Sweeping Visual Chronicle of the Sacred Female and Her Reemergence in the Cult*. New York: Harper & Row, 1989.

Gleason, Judith. *Oya: In Praise of an African Goddess*. San Francisco: Harper San Francisco, 1992.

Grant, Michael, and John Hazel. *Who's Who in Classical Mythology*. New York: Oxford University Press, 1973.

Murdock, Maureen. *Fathers' Daughters: Breaking the Ties That Bind*. New Orleans: Spring Journal Books, 1994.

Segal, Robert A., ed. *Jung on Mythology*. Princeton, NJ: Princeton University Press, 1998.

Walker, Barbara G. *The Woman's Encyclopedia of Myths and Secrets*. San Francisco: Harper & Row, 1983.

Whitmont, Edward C. *Return of the Goddess*. New York: Crossroad, 1988.

About the Author

Maureen Murdock, PhD, explores the topics of mythology and memoir through her teaching and writing. She is the author of the best-selling book *The Heroine's Journey*, which explores the rich territory of the feminine psyche. This groundbreaking book, her response to Joseph Campbell's *The Hero with a Thousand Faces*, has been translated into eighteen languages, and in 2020 Shambhala Publications issued a thirtieth-year anniversary edition with a foreword by Christine Downing. Murdock is the former chair and core faculty of the MA Counseling Psychology Program at Pacifica Graduate Institute and teaches memoir writing for the International Women's Writing Guild. She has led memoir writing retreats and workshops on *The Heroine's Journey* for women throughout the United States, Canada, Mexico, and Europe. Her other books include *Fathers' Daughters*, *The Heroine's Journey Workbook*, *Unreliable Truth*, and *Spinning Inward*. Murdock volunteers for the Alternatives to Violence Project (AVP) with inmates at Lompoc Federal Prison and lives in Santa Barbara, California.